Getting Started with Knockout.js for .NET Developers

Unleash the power of Knockout.js to build complex ASP.NET web applications

Andrey Akinshin

PUBLISHING

BIRMINGHAM - MUMBAI

Getting Started with Knockout.js for .NET Developers

First published: May 2015

Production reference: 1210515

Published by Packt Publishing Ltd.
Livery Place
35 Livery Street
Birmingham B3 2PB, UK.

ISBN 978-1-78398-400-8

www.packtpub.com

Credits

Author

Andrey Akinshin

Reviewers

Dmitry Pavlov

Tim Stuyckens

Commissioning Editor

Taron Pereira

Acquisition Editors

Owen Roberts

Greg Wild

Content Development Editors

Akshay Nair

Rohit Kumar Singh

Technical Editor

Taabish Khan

Copy Editor

Adithi Shetty

Project Coordinator

Mary Alex

Proofreaders

Safis Editing

Paul Hindle

Indexer

Priya Sane

Production Coordinator

Nitesh Thakur

Cover Work

Nitesh Thakur

About the Author

Andrey Akinshin has a PhD in computer science, and he received a Microsoft MVP award in 2015. He works as a lead .NET Developer at Perpetuum Software and as a postdoctoral research fellow at the Weizmann Institute of Science. He is also the author and main contributor of the Knockout MVC library and has a wealth of experience in Knockout.js. He has experience in various IT areas, from competitive programming (silver medal at ACM ICPC 2009) to teaching (senior lecturer and the school coach of competitive programming and mathematics teams).

You can find more information about Andrey on his home page, `http://aakinshin.net`.

About the Reviewers

Dmitry Pavlov is a 34-year-old IT guy from Saint Petersburg, Russia. He holds two degrees. His first alma mater was Saint Petersburg State University, where he graduated from the geological department with a master's degree. Then, he got interested in programming and decided to study computer science at Saint Petersburg Polytechnic State University, where he also got a master's degree. For more than 10 years, he has been involved in .NET programming at several software companies. He has held the Microsoft MVP (Visual C#) award since 2008. He has a keen interest in IT business, software development, technologies, and IT start-ups. For the last few years, he has been working as a freelance contractor and consultant, traveling with his family all over the world and enjoying his remote work.

Currently, he works as a remote ASP.NET MVC / .NET / C# developer for Toptal clients. In addition, he is a technical recruiter at Toptal (a global network of top freelance software developers).

Tim Stuyckens is a passionate web developer with several years of experience in JavaScript-heavy applications. He has been working with Knockout.js from the moment it became publicly available and since then, he has helped large .NET teams create dynamic websites. He currently works as a consultant for HR software, which is used by more than 100,000 users.

His most known open source work is the Chrome Knockout.js context debugger extension, which has more than 25,000 weekly users.

www.PacktPub.com

Support files, eBooks, discount offers, and more

For support files and downloads related to your book, please visit www.PacktPub.com.

Did you know that Packt offers eBook versions of every book published, with PDF and ePub files available? You can upgrade to the eBook version at www.PacktPub.com and as a print book customer, you are entitled to a discount on the eBook copy. Get in touch with us at service@packtpub.com for more details.

At www.PacktPub.com, you can also read a collection of free technical articles, sign up for a range of free newsletters and receive exclusive discounts and offers on Packt books and eBooks.

https://www2.packtpub.com/books/subscription/packtlib

Do you need instant solutions to your IT questions? PacktLib is Packt's online digital book library. Here, you can search, access, and read Packt's entire library of books.

Why subscribe?

- Fully searchable across every book published by Packt
- Copy and paste, print, and bookmark content
- On demand and accessible via a web browser

Free access for Packt account holders

If you have an account with Packt at www.PacktPub.com, you can use this to access PacktLib today and view 9 entirely free books. Simply use your login credentials for immediate access.

Table of Contents

Preface

Development of a big web application is a hard task. Because of this, people try to use different useful and flexible approaches to build the architecture of their applications. One such approach is Knockout.js. It is a JavaScript library that provides you with a sophisticated way to communicate between your UI and the underlying data model to create rich web user interfaces based on the Model-View-ViewModel (MVVM) pattern. Knockout.js provides a simple two-way data binding mechanism between your data model and UI, which means that any change to your data model is automatically reflected in the UI and vice versa. Instead of using pure Knockout.js, you can use Knockout MVC. It is a library for ASP.NET MVC, which is a wrapper for Knockout.js that helps to move the entire business logic to the server side; the complete JavaScript code necessary on the client side will be generated.

This book will provide you with the skills you need to successfully create a Knockout.js-based application of varying complexity, from a simple Knockout.js web page in pure JavaScript to a complex ASP.NET web application. You will learn how you can use the MVVM design pattern, including the dependency tracking system and observable properties for creation of powerful sites with a clear separation of model, logic, and view layers.

What this book covers

Chapter 1, *Introduction to Knockout.js*, teaches basic Knockout.js concepts (overview), such as MVVM design pattern (including the creation of Model, ViewModel, and View), binding, observables, and subscribe machinery. Also, we'll consider an installation process for the library.

Chapter 2, *Creating a Simple Knockout.js Application*, covers how to use advanced Knockout.js features, such as working with observables arrays, special bindings, and computed observables.

Chapter 3, Integrating Knockout.js in ASP.NET MVC Applications, uses our Knockout.js experience to create a simple ASP.NET MVC application. We'll create a simple application in pure Knockout.js + ASP.NET MVC without external libraries. We'll cover how to create a Model in C# and connect it with the MVVM structure in JavaScript.

Chapter 4, Creating a Web Application with Knockout MVC, discusses how to move the entire business logic to the server side; the complete JavaScript code necessary on the client side will be generated automatically based on the described C# (or VB.NET) model.

Chapter 5, Advanced Features of Knockout.js, covers how to use advanced Knockout MVC features. The basic set will be enough for a very simple application. Any real application needs special concepts, such as regions, complex bindings, combined contexts, and so on. You may need to transfer some parameters to the server, write your own user scripts, or perform lazy loading of your data in the case of big data.

Chapter 6, Advanced Features of Knockout MVC, discusses how to use advanced Knockout MVC features. The basic set will be enough for a very simple application. Any real application needs special concepts, such as regions, complex bindings, combined contexts, and so on. You may need to transfer some parameters to the server, write your own user scripts, or make lazy loading of your data in the big data case.

Appendix, A Brief on Knockout MVC References and Features, lists some references and features that will be useful to readers.

What you need for this book

For this book, you need to have the following software set up:

- Web browser: Internet Explorer, Mozilla Firefox, or Google Chrome
- Text editor: Notepad++ or Sublime Text
- C# IDE with ASP.NET support: Visual Studio C# Express or Visual Studio Community

You can work on Windows, Mac OS, or Linux.

Who this book is for

This book is intended for .NET developers who want to use the MVVM design pattern to create a powerful client-side JavaScript linked to server-side C# logic. Basic experience with ASP.NET, Razor, and creating web applications is needed. Also, elementary knowledge of C# or JavaScript is expected.

Conventions

In this book, you will find a number of text styles that distinguish between different kinds of information. Here are some examples of these styles and an explanation of their meaning.

Code words in text, database table names, folder names, filenames, file extensions, pathnames, dummy URLs, user input, and Twitter handles are shown as follows: "The model has two additional methods: `GetName` and `GetBooks`."

A block of code is set as follows:

```
var self = this;
self.Name = ko.observable();
self.Books = ko.observableArray();
```

When we wish to draw your attention to a particular part of a code block, the relevant lines or items are set in bold:

```
var PersonViewModel = function() {
  var self = this;
  self.children = ko.observableArray(person.children);
  self.selectedChildren = ko.observable([]);
```

Any command-line input or output is written as follows:

```
PM> Install-Package bootstrap
```

New terms and **important words** are shown in bold. Words that you see on the screen, for example, in menus or dialog boxes, appear in the text like this: "In our case, we need to select the **Empty MVC controller** template."

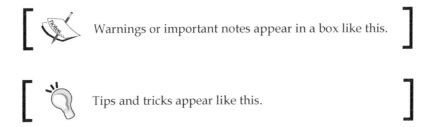

Warnings or important notes appear in a box like this.

Tips and tricks appear like this.

Reader feedback

Feedback from our readers is always welcome. Let us know what you think about this book—what you liked or disliked. Reader feedback is important for us as it helps us develop titles that you will really get the most out of.

To send us general feedback, simply e-mail feedback@packtpub.com, and mention the book's title in the subject of your message.

If there is a topic that you have expertise in and you are interested in either writing or contributing to a book, see our author guide at www.packtpub.com/authors.

Customer support

Now that you are the proud owner of a Packt book, we have a number of things to help you to get the most from your purchase.

Downloading the example code

You can download the example code files from your account at http://www.packtpub.com for all the Packt Publishing books you have purchased. If you purchased this book elsewhere, you can visit http://www.packtpub.com/support and register to have the files e-mailed directly to you.

Errata

Although we have taken every care to ensure the accuracy of our content, mistakes do happen. If you find a mistake in one of our books—maybe a mistake in the text or the code—we would be grateful if you could report this to us. By doing so, you can save other readers from frustration and help us improve subsequent versions of this book. If you find any errata, please report them by visiting http://www.packtpub.com/submit-errata, selecting your book, clicking on the **Errata Submission Form** link, and entering the details of your errata. Once your errata are verified, your submission will be accepted and the errata will be uploaded to our website or added to any list of existing errata under the Errata section of that title.

To view the previously submitted errata, go to https://www.packtpub.com/books/content/support and enter the name of the book in the search field. The required information will appear under the **Errata** section.

Piracy

Piracy of copyrighted material on the Internet is an ongoing problem across all media. At Packt, we take the protection of our copyright and licenses very seriously. If you come across any illegal copies of our works in any form on the Internet, please provide us with the location address or website name immediately so that we can pursue a remedy.

Please contact us at copyright@packtpub.com with a link to the suspected pirated material.

We appreciate your help in protecting our authors and our ability to bring you valuable content.

Questions

If you have a problem with any aspect of this book, you can contact us at questions@packtpub.com, and we will do our best to address the problem.

1
Introduction to Knockout.js

Knockout.js is a popular JavaScript library that allows easy creation of powerful web applications based on the **Model-View-ViewModel** (**MVVM**) design pattern.

In this chapter, we will cover the following topics:

- Knockout.js overview
- Installing Knockout.js
- Knockout.js fundamentals

Knockout.js overview

In this section, we will take a look at Knockout.js, including a brief introduction and the best features. If you already have some experience with the library, then you can skip this chapter and go to *Chapter 2, Creating a Simple Knockout.js Application*, to read about the advanced features.

What is Knockout.js?

Knockout.js is an open source standalone JavaScript library developed by Steve Sanderson in 2010. The main concept of the library is implementation of the Model-View-ViewModel design pattern for web applications on the client side. The library has powerful tools to make your JavaScript code and HTML/CSS markup easier and more readable with the help of so-called **observables objects** and **declarative bindings**.

Thus Knockout.js can help you create rich HTML pages with a clean underlying data model and dynamically self-updatable UI even for very big applications with complex logic and interfaces.

The best features

Knockout.js has a lot of features that distinguish it from other similar JavaScript frameworks. There are different solutions to create the common logic of your application and interaction between data and user interface. When you select the main library to build an application, you should understand its benefits.

The following are the best features of Knockout.js:

- **Nice dependency tracking based on MVVM**: Once data is changed, HTML will be automatically updated. You shouldn't think about updating DOM when writing logic code. We will discuss the MVVM pattern in more detail later.

- **Two-way declarative bindings**: This is a very simple way to link DOM elements to your data model, as shown in the following line of code:

```
<button data-bind="enable: items().count
  < 7">Add</button><input data-bind="value: username" />
```

- **Simple and extensible**: You can write your own type of declarative bindings for any purpose. Each new binding is defined by two simple functions for the init and update events. For example, you can define a binding for the duration of a slide animation, as follows:

```
<div data-bind="slideDuration: 600">Content</div>
```

- **Absence of dependency**: You don't need any third-party libraries. However, you may need the jQuery library for some advanced features support or performance issues, but most applications already use this library.

- **Pure JavaScript**: Knockout.js doesn't use any JavaScript superstructure, such as TypeScript or CoffeeScript. The source code of the library is represented by the pure and readable JavaScript code; it works with any server- or client-side technology.

- **Compatibility with mainstream browsers**: Knockout.js supports Mozilla Firefox 2+, Google Chrome 5+, Opera 10+, Safari, and even Internet Explorer 6+. It also works excellently on mobile (phone and tablet) devices.

- **Small size**: The size of Knockout.js is around 46 KB after gzipping for version 3.1.0. The debug versions (without compression) have a size of around 214 KB but you don't need it in the production case.

- **Templating**: The powerful template system will allow you to create reusable HTML chunks, which you can use for parts of a web page. It also has a nice syntax, as shown in the following code:

```
<script type="text/html" id="person-template">
    <h3 data-bind="text: name"></h3>
    <p>Credits: <span data-bind="text: credits"></span></p>
</script>
```

MVVM design pattern

The Model-View-ViewModel is a design pattern with a clear separation of the user interface from business logic. The main components of MVVM are as follows:

- **Model**: This represents the state and operations of your business objects and is independent of UI. When using Knockout.js, you will usually make Ajax calls to some server-side code to read and write this stored model data.
- **View**: This is a visible UI representing your business objects.
- **ViewModel**: This is an intermediary between the View and Model, and is responsible for handling the UI logic.

You can see the scheme of MVVM in the following diagram:

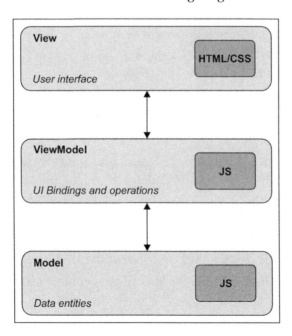

The MVVM pattern looks like the classic **Model-View-Controller** (**MVC**) pattern. The Model is also your stored data, the View is also a graphical representation of your data for the user, but instead of a controller, MVVM uses a ViewModel for interaction between the Model and View. The MVVM has a number of advantages over the MVC, such as the following:

- **Low coupling**: It's a property of the MVVM by design, because of which we use a clearer separation between the data, interface, and behavior. MVVM has a clearer separation between the data, interface, and behavior for most application architectures.

- **Testable**: Low coupling makes the application more comfortable for unit-testing; now you can separately test each layer of your application. Testing UI logic by testing only ViewModel is an easier way than testing a complete HTML page.

- **Code extensibility**: Separation by layers makes it easier to extend each specific part of the code without affecting the others.

- **Two-way data-binding**: This avoids having to write a lot of boilerplate code.

Let's consider MVVM in examples. In parentheses, you can see the representation format of each layer, but note that these are just examples; different applications use different formats:

- **Knockout.js**: This is the target case for this book. Most often, a Knockout.js application will use the following schemes:
  - **Model**: This includes some data on the server side; you can read and write it via Ajax calls (JSON).
  - **View**: This is the web page (HTML/CSS).
  - **ViewModel**: This is the representation of data and operations (JavaScript).

- **WPF**: Many .NET developers are familiar with MVVM on technologies such as WPF, Silverlight, and WinRT. Originally, the MVVM pattern was conceived to support WPF and Silverlight. For example, you can use the following scheme in your WPF application:
  - **Model**: This includes some data in the client database (binary)
  - **View**: This is the user interface of the WPF application (XAML)
  - **ViewModel**: This is the special data context classes (C#)

In this book, we will not explain MVVM in detail because the easiest way to understand MVVM is a careful study of the examples in this book. The examples will work only with View and ViewModel because communication with a real data model (commonly, some data on the server, which can use SQL, RSS, XML, binary, and so on) is another story. Within these examples, you can consider the ViewModel as the Model as well because it actually holds all your data. In a real application, you should select a way to transfer this data to the server.

Installing Knockout.js

There are a few ways to install Knockout.js, and each method is outlined here. Generally, you want to use the first or second method, but the third and fourth methods can be useful in some special cases.

Method 1 – official site

You can manually download Knockout.js from the official site `http://knockoutjs.com/`. You can see the screen of the main page in the following screenshot:

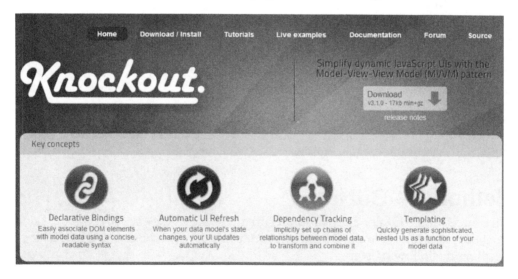

After downloading, you can add a reference to Knockout.js from your HTML page using a `<script>` tag. For example, if the library was downloaded to the root directory of your application, then you can use the following line of code:

```
<script type='text/javascript' src='knockout-3.1.0.js'></script>
```

You should use the actual version of the library instead of version 3.1.0 (released in March 2014) in the preceding example line of code. Hereafter, we will use version 3.1.0 (it is the current version at the time of writing this book), but because of backward compatibility all examples should work with future Knockout.js versions very well.

Also, you can download the debug build for learning purposes (from the download page at `http://knockoutjs.com/downloads/index.html`). It helps you to understand how Knockout.js works. Don't use it for real production applications.

Method 2 – NuGet

If you develop a website with .NET, you can install it via NuGet (`https://www.nuget.org/packages/knockoutjs`). Just run the following command in the Package Manager Console:

```
Install-Package knockoutjs
```

Method 3 – CDNs

Content distribution network (CDN) is a large system for delivery or distribution of some content to end users' servers. You can use third-party CDNs for reference Knockout.js. Examples of CDNs can be found at `http://cdnjs.cloudflare.com/ajax/libs/knockout/3.1.0/knockout-min.js` and `http://ajax.aspnetcdn.com/ajax/knockout/knockout-3.0.0.js`.

Note that not all CDNs support the latest actual version of the library. The best way is to use a local library version on your server, but the CDNs method can be very useful for quick single-page solutions.

Method 4 – GitHub

Full sources of the library are placed on GitHub at `https://github.com/knockout/knockout`. You can build the latest Knockout.js version from source by yourself by executing the following steps:

1. Clone the repo from GitHub. Make sure that you have Git installed on your local machine:

   ```
   git clone https://github.com/knockout/knockout.git
   cd knockout
   ```

2. Acquire build dependencies. Make sure that you have Node.js installed on your local machine:

```
npm install -g grunt-cli
npm install
```

3. Run the build tool:

```
Grunt
```

Done! Now you can find the built files in the `build/output/` directory.

Knockout.js fundamentals

In this section, you will learn how to create a very simple "Hello World" application with step-by-step instructions. Each step will describe one of the main Knockout.js concepts.

Creating a View

Let's learn about Knockout.js with a very simple example. We start work with the following code of an HTML page (`HelloWorld-Example1.html`):

```html
<!DOCTYPE html>
<html lang="en">
  <head>
    <meta charset="utf-8" />
    <title>Hello world on Knockout.js</title>
  </head>
<body>
<span>Hello World!</span>

<script type='text/javascript' src='knockout-3.1.0.js'></script>
</body>
</html>
```

If we open this page in our favorite web browser, we will see the blank page with a single line, **Hello World!**. The body of this HTML page is the View layer of our MVVM pattern.

However, we did not use Knockout.js in this example. Let's change it.

Adding a ViewModel

Let's add some JavaScript code to our example. We will move information about the printed string from the View layer (HTML page) to the ViewModel layer (JavaScript object):

```
<script type='text/javascript'>
  var viewModel = {
    message: "Hello world!"
  };
  ko.applyBindings(viewModel);
</script>
```

In this example, the `viewModel` is a simple JavaScript object with a single message property. In the last line of the script, we activated Knockout.js by the `applyBindings` method of a global Knockout.js object called `ko`. The first parameter takes the ViewModel object that you want to use.

It's time to connect ViewModel with our HTML.

Adding a data binding

Let's change the inline `Hello World!` string to an empty span element with data binding (the full code of the page is placed in `HelloWorld-Example2.html`):

```
<span data-bind="text: message"></span>
```

The syntax of Knockout's declarative bindings provides a powerful way to link your data (the View) with your UI (the ViewModel). You can see an example of such syntax in the preceding HTML line; it consists of two parts (as a value of the `data-bind` property), the binding name and value, separated by a colon. In the example, we bind the `text` property of the `span` element to the user-defined `message` property of ViewModel.

Because of the `message` property, the content of the `span` element is `Hello world!`. The rendered HTML page is still represented by a single text line.

Adding an observable

Now our example has one thing lacking: changes of the ViewModel don't link to changes of the View. We can improve the situation with observables. Let's update the `viewModel` definition (see `HelloWorld-Example3.html`):

```
var viewModel = {
  message: ko.observable()
```

```
};
viewModel.message("Hello world!");
ko.applyBindings(viewModel);
```

In this example, message is an observable property. It means that after any changes to the message property, UI elements with corresponding bindings will be automatically updated.

You should understand that the ko.observable properties are actually functions. Therefore, you can use these functions to read and write. If you want to write some value in a property, you should call an observable function with a new value as the first parameter (such as in the preceding listing). If you want to read a value from a property, you should call the observable function without any parameters:

```
viewModel.message("Hello, world!");   // Write operation
currentMessage = viewModel.message(); // Read operation
```

The observables are the most important part of the Knockout.js MVVM structures. All of your ViewModel properties that are involved in the UI update process should be defined as an observable (such as in the preceding code via ko.observable). A non-observable property will work only for one-time read-only data binding. It may be useful for some special cases, but generally, you should describe all of your ViewModel properties as observables.

Also, you can set the initial observable value directly in the definition (for example, message: ko.observable("Hello world!")).

Subscribing to observables

Most applications don't need an explicit way to subscribe to observables (such operations are performed implicitly using the declarative style), but in some special scenarios, it may be useful. Now we consider the explicit way for a better understanding of the observables concept.

Explicitly subscribing means declaring a callback with the subscribe function, as shown in the following example (see HelloWorld-Example4.html):

```
viewModel.message.subscribe(function(newValue) {
  alert("New message is " + newValue);
})
```

After this subscription, any changes to the message property would entail an alert message about the changes.

In a real application, it may be useful to create an additional logic for the observable property change event that you can't make by the usual declarative bindings.

Updating View in a forced way

A data binding can have additional properties. Let's consider an example. By default, the View layer gets a notification about data changes only if the data was actually changed. However, we can modify this behavior and make ViewModel always send notifications. For this purpose, you will use the so-called `notify` extender to ensure that our subscribers are always notified on a write request, even if the new property value is the same:

```
viewModel.message.extend({ notify: 'always' });
```

In the preceding line of code (see `HelloWorld-Example5.html`), we call the `extend` function to update the `notify` property of `message` by the `always` value.

In a real application, it may be useful if you want to notify a user about any change operation of data, regardless of a new value.

Delaying and suppressing change notifications

Let's consider another extender example. Normally, an observable notifies its subscribers immediately, as soon as it's changed. However, if an observable is changed repeatedly or triggers expensive updates, you may get better performance by limiting or delaying the observable's change notifications, as follows:

```
viewModel.message.extend({ rateLimit: 100 });
```

In the preceding line of code (see `HelloWorld-Example6.html`), we call the `extend` function to update the `rateLimit` property of `message` by `100`. It means that ViewModel will notify the View about changes no more than once in every 100 milliseconds.

Adding dynamic behavior

It's time for a more interesting example. We will add some dynamic behavior. Let's insert a button to add an exclamation mark to our message. The new representation of the View layer will be as follows:

```
<span data-bind="text: message"></span><br />
<button data-bind="click: addExclamationMark">Add exclamation
  mark</button>
```

The representation of the ViewModel layer will be as follows:

```
var viewModel = {
  message: ko.observable(),
  addExclamationMark : function() {
    this.message(this.message() + "!")
  }
};
viewModel.message("Hello world!");
ko.applyBindings(viewModel);
```

In the View, we can see the button with the new declarative binding: `click`. This binding expression sets the `click` button event handler to `addExclamationMark`. We can find the declaration of this function in the ViewModel:

```
addExclamationMark : function() {
  this.message(this.message() + "!")
}
```

In the body of the function, we used the `message` property twice: once to read and once to write. More specifically, we took the current value of `message`, added an exclamation mark to the obtained string value, and set the composite string as the new `message` value.

Try to run the example (`HelloWorld-Example7.html`) and click on the button. You will see how the message is modified, as shown in the following screenshot:

A binding diversity

There are different ways to use Knockout.js declarative bindings. We will consider it in the following chapters, but for now, you can briefly look at the following binding example to understand the diversity of opportunities that you have with Knockout.js. You can find the full list of examples with comments in the `BindingDiversity.html` file.

Single and multiple bindings

An element can use a single binding (described by the name and value) or multiple bindings (related and unrelated). In the last case, each binding should be separated from the previous one by a comma:

```
<!-- Single -->
<span data-bind="text: message"></span>

<!-- Multiple related -->
<input data-bind="value: name, valueUpdate: 'afterkeydown'" />

<!-- Multiple unrelated -->
<input data-bind="value: name, enable: isNameEnable" />
```

Value representation

The value of a binding can be represented by a single value, variable, or literal. In addition, you can use some JavaScript expressions, including function calls, as shown in the following code:

```
<!-- Variable -->
<div data-bind="visible: shouldShowMessage">...</div>

<!-- Simple expression + value -->
<span data-bind="text: price() > 50 ? 'expensive' :
  'cheap'"></span>

<!-- Functional call -->
<button data-bind="enable: parseAreaCode(cellphoneNumber()) !==
  '555'">...</button>

<!-- Function expression -->
<div data-bind="click: function (data) { myFunction('param1',
  data) }">...</div>

<!-- Object literal -->
<div data-bind="with: {emotion: 'happy', 'facial-expression':
  'smile'}">...</div>
```

Note that such examples demonstrate a kind of bad practice because the good way encapsulates all the logic in the ViewModel layer.

White spaces

White spaces (spaces, tabs, and newlines) do not affect bindings. The following examples are all equivalent:

```
<!-- Without spaces -->
<select data-bind="options:availableCountries,optionsText:'countryName
',value:selectedCountry,optionsCaption:'Choose...'"></select>

<!-- With spaces -->
<select data-bind="options : availableCountries, optionsText
: 'countryName', value : selectedCountry, optionsCaption :
'Choose...'"></select>

<!-- With newlines -->
<select data-bind="
    options: availableCountries,
    optionsText: 'countryName',
    value: selectedCountry,
    optionsCaption: 'Choose...'"></select>
```

Skipping the value

If you use Knockout.js 3.0+, you can use the binding without a value, as shown in the following code. In this case, binding will have an undefined value. It can be useful with **binding preprocessing** (you will learn about this feature in future chapters):

```
<!-- Without a value -->
<span data-bind="text">Text that will be cleared when bindings are
  applied.</span>
```

Useful links

You can find more useful information about Knockout.js at the following links:

- **Official site**: http://knockoutjs.com/
- **Documentation**: http://knockoutjs.com/documentation/introduction.html
- **Tutorials**: http://learn.knockoutjs.com/
- **Live examples**: http://knockoutjs.com/examples/
- **Forum**: https://groups.google.com/forum/#!forum/knockoutjs
- **Source code**: https://github.com/knockout/knockout

Information about Knockout.js developers can be found at the following links:

- **Steven Sanderson's blog**: http://blog.stevensanderson.com/
- **Steven Sanderson's Twitter**: https://twitter.com/stevensanderson
- **Ryan Niemeyer's blog**: http://www.knockmeout.net/
- **Ryan Niemeyer's Twitter**: https://twitter.com/RPNiemeyer

> **Downloading the example code**
>
> You can download the example code files from your account at http://www.packtpub.com for all the Packt Publishing books you have purchased. If you purchased this book elsewhere, you can visit http://www.packtpub.com/support and register to have the files e-mailed directly to you.

Summary

In this chapter, we got acquainted with Knockout.js, what it is what its benefits are, how to download and install it, and how to write a simple "Hello World" application. In addition, we covered the MVVM design pattern and how it helps us to build a nice application with the help of Knockout.js. The Hello World example demonstrates basic Knockout.js features, such as observables, data bindings, subscribing logic, and its extenders.

2
Creating a Simple Knockout.js Application

In this chapter, we'll create a simple Knockout.js application in pure JavaScript, which uses the fundamental concepts from *Chapter 1, Introduction to Knockout.js*. Also, we'll discuss how to use advanced Knockout.js features, such as working with special bindings, and computed observables.

This experience is needed to create any Knockout.js application of medium level. Also, it's needed to understand client-server interaction in real ASP.NET MVC applications.

We will cover the following topics in this chapter:

- Text and appearance bindings
- Form field bindings
- Control flow bindings
- Computed observables
- Observable arrays

Creating the Model, View, and ViewModel

In this chapter, we will develop a **Single Page Application** (**SPA**) with information about a person. Let's call it the "Personal" page. Before we begin to analyze examples, we need to do some preparatory work.

In *Chapter 1, Introduction to Knockout.js,* we examined the **MVVM (Model-View-ViewModel)** design pattern. For a better understanding of this approach to application architecture, we will split each example into three parts, corresponding to the three layers of MVVM.

In a real application, the data will be placed on the server (the Model layer of our MVVM pattern), but we will not consider client-server interaction. So, let's assume that the Model layer is a separated JavaScript object. All operations (such as viewing and editing) will be performed with data in the ViewModel, without any relation to the server. Let's start with a simple blank HTML page (`PersonalPage-Blank.html`):

```
<!DOCTYPE html>
<html lang="en">
  <head>
    <meta charset="utf-8" />
    <title>Personal page</title>
  </head>
<body>

<!-- View will be here -->

<script type="text/javascript" src="knockout-3.1.0.js"></script>
<script type="text/javascript">
// Model
var person = {
};
// ViewModel
var PersonViewModel = function() {
  var self = this;
};
// Apply
ko.applyBindings(PersonViewModel);
</script>
</html>
```

In the preceding code, the `person` JavaScript object plays the Model role of our application, and `PersonViewModel` plays the ViewModel role. We could have merged ViewModel and Model (in this case, the ViewModel will contain data), but we did it strictly to understand the MVVM pattern. Also, we will not consider the interaction between the Model and ViewModel; we will describe the `person` object only to highlight data that should be contained in the Model. In the examples that follow, the Model will contain some initial information about a person. As an example rule, we will work with a fictional character, John Doe.

You should note that the ViewModel is created with the help of a function. The one good practice is avoiding the need to track `this`. Instead of `this`, the ViewModel constructor copies a reference to `this` to a special variable `self` (for more information, see *JavaScript: The Good Parts, Douglas Crockford, O'Reilly Media*). Now you can use `self` throughout the ViewModel and not worry about referring the variable to something else.

In each section of this chapter, we will discuss some features of Knockout.js and how we can use it in our Personal page.

Text and appearance bindings

Knockout.js provides you with a huge number of useful HTML data bindings to control the text and its appearance. In *Chapter 1, Introduction to Knockout.js*, we discussed what bindings are and how we can use them. In this section, we take a brief look at the most common ones:

- The `text` binding
- The `html` binding
- The `css` binding
- The `style` binding
- The `attr` binding
- The `visible` binding

The text binding

The `text` binding is one of the most useful bindings. It allows us to bind `text` of an element (for example, `span`) to a property of the ViewModel. Let's create an example in which a person has a single `firstName` property (`PersonalPage-Binding-Text1.html`).

The **Model** will be as follows:

```
var person = {
  firstName: "John"
};
```

The **ViewModel** will be as follows:

```
var PersonViewModel = function() {
  var self = this;
  self.firstName = ko.observable(person.firstName);
};
```

The **View** will be as follows:

```
The first name is <span data-bind="text: firstName"></span>.
```

It is really a very simple example. The Model (the `person` object) has only the `firstName` property with the initial value `John`. In the ViewModel, we created the `firstName` property, which is represented by `ko.observable`. The View contains a `span` element with a single data binding; the `text` property of `span` binds to the `firstName` property of the ViewModel. In this example, any changes to `personViewModel.firstName` will entail an automatic update of `text` in the `span` element. If we run the example, we will see a single text line: **The first name is John.**

Let's upgrade our example by adding the `age` property for the person. In the View, we will print **young person** for `age` less than 18 or **adult person** for `age` greater than or equal to 18 (`PersonalPage-Binding-Text2.html`):

The **Model** will be as follows:

```
var person = {
  firstName: "John",
  age: 30
};
```

The **ViewModel** will be as follows:

```
var personViewModel = function() {
  var self = this;
  self.firstName = ko.observable(person.firstName);
  self.age = ko.observable(person.age);
};
```

The **View** will be as follows:

```
<span data-bind="text: firstName"></span> is <span data-
  bind="text: age() >= 18 ? 'adult' : 'young'"></span>
  person.
```

This example uses an expression binding in the View. The second `span` element binds its `text` property to a JavaScript expression. In this case, we will see the text **John is adult person** because we set `age` to `30` in the Model.

> Note that it is bad practice to write expressions such as `age() >= 18` directly inside the binding value. The best way is to define the so-called **computed observable property** that contains a boolean expression and uses the name of the defined property instead of the expression. We will discuss this method later.

The html binding

In some cases, we may want to use HTML tags inside our data binding. However, if we include HTML tags in the `text` binding, tags will be shown in the raw form. We should use the `html` binding to render tags, as shown in the following example (`PersonalPage-Binding-Html.html`):

The **Model** will be as follows:

```
var person = {
  about: "John's favorite site is <a
    href='http://www.packtpub.com'>PacktPub</a>."
};
```

The **ViewModel** will be as follows:

```
var PersonViewModel = function() {
  var self = this;
  self.about = ko.observable(person.about);
};
```

The **View** will be as follows:

```
<span data-bind="html: about"></span>
```

Thanks to the `html` binding, the `about` message will be displayed correctly and the `<a>` tag will be transformed into a hyperlink. When you try to display a link with the `text` binding, the HTML will be encoded, so the user will see not a link but special characters.

The css binding

The html binding is a good way to include HTML tags in the binding value, but it is a bad practice for its styling. Instead of this, we should use the css binding for this aim. Let's consider the following example (PersonalPage-Binding-Css.html):

The **Model** will be as follows:

```
var person = {
  favoriteColor: "red"
};
```

The **ViewModel** will be as follows:

```
var PersonViewModel = function() {
  var self = this;
  self.favoriteColor = ko.observable(person.favoriteColor);
};
```

The **View** will be as follows:

```
<style type="text/css">
  .redStyle {
    color: red;
  }
  .greenStyle {
    color: green;
  }
</style>
<div data-bind="css: { redStyle: favoriteColor() == 'red',
  greenStyle: favoriteColor() == 'green' }">
John's favorite color is <span data-bind="text:
  favoriteColor"></span>.
</div>
```

In the View, there are two CSS classes: redStyle and greenStyle. In the Model, we use favoriteColor to define the favorite color of our person. The expression binding for the div element applies the redStyle CSS style for red color and greenStyle for green color. It uses the favoriteColor observable property as a function to get its value. When favoriteColor is not an observable, the data binding will just be favoriteColor== 'red'. Of course, when favoriteColor changes, the DOM will not be updated because it won't be notified.

The style binding

In some cases, we do not have access to CSS, but we still need to change the style of the View. For example, CSS files are placed in an application theme and we may not have enough rights to modify it. The style binding helps us in such a case (PersonalPage-Binding-Style.html):

The **Model** will be as follows:

```
var person = {
  favoriteColor: "red"
};
```

The **ViewModel** will be as follows:

```
var PersonViewModel = function() {
  var self = this;
  self.favoriteColor = ko.observable(person.favoriteColor);
};
```

The **View** will be as follows:

```
<div data-bind="style: { color: favoriteColor() }">
John's favorite color is <span data-bind="text:
  favoriteColor"></span>.
</div>
```

This example is analogous to the previous one, with the only difference being that we use the style binding instead of the css binding.

The attr binding

The attr binding is also a good way to work with DOM elements. It allows us to set the value of any attributes of elements. Let's look at the following example (PersonalPage-Binding-Attr.html):

The **Model** will be as follows:

```
var person = {
  favoriteUrl: "http://www.packtpub.com"
};
```

The **ViewModel** will be as follows:

```
var PersonViewModel = function() {
  var self = this;
  self.favoriteUrl = ko.observable(person.favoriteUrl);
};
```

The **View** will be as follows:

```
John's favorite site is <a data-bind="attr: { href: favoriteUrl()
  }">PacktPub</a>.
```

The `href` attribute of the `<a>` element binds to the `favoriteUrl` property of the ViewModel via the `attr` binding.

The visible binding

The `visible` binding allows us to show or hide some elements according to the ViewModel. Let's consider an example with a `div` element, which is shown depending on a conditional binding (`PersonalPage-Binding-Visible.html`):

The **Model** will be as follows:

```
var person = {
  favoriteSite: "PacktPub"
};
```

The **ViewModel** will be as follows:

```
var PersonViewModel = function() {
  var self = this;
  self.favoriteSite = ko.observable(person.favoriteSite);
};
```

The **View** will be as follows:

```
<div data-bind="visible: favoriteSite().length > 0">
John's favorite site is <span data-bind="text:
  favoriteSite"></span>.
</div>
```

In this example, the `div` element with information about John's favorite site will be shown only if the information was defined.

Form fields bindings

Forms are important parts of many web applications. In this section, we will learn about a number of data bindings to work with the form fields:

- The `value` binding
- The `click` binding
- The `submit` binding
- The `event` binding
- The `checked` binding
- The `enable` binging
- The `disable` binding
- The `options` binding
- The `selectedOptions` binding

The value binding

Very often, forms use the `input`, `select` and `textarea` elements to enter text. Knockout.js allows work with such text via the `value` binding, as shown in the following example (`PersonalPage-Binding-Value.html`):

The **Model** will be as follows:

```
var person = {
  firstName: "John"
};
```

The **ViewModel** will be as follows:

```
var PersonViewModel = function() {
  var self = this;
  self.firstName = ko.observable(person.firstName);
};
```

The **View** will be as follows:

```
<form>
  The first name is <input type="text" data-bind="value:
    firstName" />.
</form>
```

The `value` property of the text `input` element binds to the `firstName` property of the ViewModel.

The click binding

We can add some function as an event handler for the onclick event with the click binding. Let's consider the following example (PersonalPage-Binding-Click.html):

The **Model** will be as follows:

```
var person = {
  age: 30
};
```

The **ViewModel** will be as follows:

```
var personViewModel = function() {
  var self = this;
  self.age = ko.observable(person.age);
  self.growOld = function() {
    var previousAge = self.age();
    self.age(previousAge + 1);
  }
};
```

The **View** will be as follows:

```
<div>
  John's age is <span data-bind="text: age"></span>.
  <button data-bind="click: growOld">Grow old</button>
</div>
```

We have the **Grow old** button in the View. The click property of this button binds to the growOld function of the ViewModel. This function increases the age of the person by one year. Because the age property is an observable, the text in the span element will automatically be updated to 31.

The submit binding

Typically, the submit event is the last operation when working with a form. Knockout.js supports the submit binding to add the corresponding event handler. Of course, you can also use the click binding for the "submit" button, but that is a different thing because there are alternative ways to submit the form. For example, a user can use the *Enter* key while typing into a textbox.

Let's update the previous example with the `submit` binding (`PersonalPage-Binding-Submit.html`):

The **Model** will be as follows:

```
var person = {
  age: 30
};
```

The **ViewModel** will be as follows:

```
var PersonViewModel = function() {
  var self = this;
  self.age = ko.observable(person.age);
  self.growOld = function() {
    var previousAge = self.age();
    self.age(previousAge + 1);
  }
};
```

The **View** will be as follows:

```
<div>
  John's age is <span data-bind="text: age"></span>.
  <form data-bind="submit: growOld">
    <button type="submit">Grow old</button>
  </form>
</div>
```

The only new thing is moving the link to the `growOld` function to the `submit` binding of the form.

The event binding

The `event` binding also helps us interact with the user. This binding allows us to add an event handler to an element, events such as `keypress`, `mouseover`, or `mouseout`. In the following example, we use this binding to control the visibility of a `div` element according to the mouse position (`PersonalPage-Binding-Event.html`):

The **Model** will be as follows:

```
var person = {
};
```

The **ViewModel** will be as follows:

```
var PersonViewModel = function() {
  var self = this;
  self.aboutEnabled = ko.observable(false);
  self.showAbout = function() {
    self.aboutEnabled(true);
  };
  self.hideAbout = function() {
    self.aboutEnabled(false);
  }
};
```

The **View** will be as follows:

```
<div>
  <div data-bind="event: { mouseover: showAbout, mouseout:
    hideAbout }">
    Mouse over to view the information about John.
  </div>
  <div data-bind="visible: aboutEnabled">
    John's favorite site is <a
      href='http://www.packtpub.com'>PacktPub</a>.
  </div>
</div>
```

In this example, the Model is empty because the web page doesn't have a state outside of the runtime context. The single property aboutEnabled makes sense only to run an application. In such a case, we can omit the corresponding property in the Model and work only with the ViewModel. In particular, we will work with a single ViewModel property aboutEnabled, which defines the visibility of div. There are two event bindings: mouseover and mouseout. They link the mouse behavior to the value of aboutEnabled with the help of the showAbout and hideAbout ViewModel functions.

The checked binding

Many forms contain checkboxes (<input type="checkbox" />). We can work with its value with the help of the checked binding, as shown in the following example (PersonalPage-Binding-Checked.html):

The **Model** will be as follows:

```
var person = {
  isMarried: false
};
```

The **ViewModel** will be as follows:

```
var personViewModel = function() {
  var self = this;
  self.isMarried = ko.observable(person.isMarried);
};
```

The **View** is as follows:

```
<form>
  <input type="checkbox" data-bind="checked: isMarried" />
  Is married
</form>
```

The View contains the **Is married** checkbox. Its checked property binds to the Boolean isMarried property of the ViewModel.

The enable and disable binding

A good usability practice suggests setting the enable property of some elements (such as input, select, and textarea) according to a form state. Knockout.js provides us with the enable binding for this purpose. Let's consider the following example (PersonalPage-Binding-Enable.html):

The **Model** is as follows:

```
var person = {
  isMarried: false,
  wife: ""
};
```

The **ViewModel** will be as follows:

```
var PersonViewModel = function() {
  var self = this;
  self.isMarried = ko.observable(person.isMarried);
  self.wife = ko.observable(person.wife);
};
```

The View will be as follows:

```
<form>
  <p>
    <input type="checkbox" data-bind="checked: isMarried" />
    Is married
```

```
    </p>
    <p>
      Wife's name:
      <input type="text" data-bind="value: wife, enable: isMarried" />
    </p>
  </form>
```

The View contains the checkbox from the previous example. Only in the case of a married person can we write the name of his wife. This behavior is provided by the `enable` binding of the text `input` element.

The `disable` binding works in exactly the opposite way. It allows you to avoid negative expression bindings in some cases.

The options binding

If the Model contains some collections, then we need a `select` element to display it. The `options` binding allows us to link such an element to the data, as shown in the following example (`PersonalPage-Binding-Options.html`):

The **Model** is as follows:

```
var person = {
  children: ["Jonnie", "Jane", "Richard", "Mary"]
};
```

The **ViewModel** will be as follows:

```
var PersonViewModel = function() {
  var self = this;
  self.children = person.children;
};
```

The **View** will be as follows:

```
<form>
  <select multiple="multiple" data-bind="options:
    children"></select>
</form>
```

In the preceding example, the Model contains the `children` array. The View represents this array with the help of multiple `select` elements. Note that, in this example, `children` is a non-observable array. Therefore, changes to ViewModel in this case do not affect the View. The code is shown only for demonstration of the `options` binding. Observable arrays will be discussed in detail in future sections.

The selectedOptions binding

In addition to the `options` binding, we can use the `selectedOptions` binding to work with selected items in the `select` element. Let's look at the following example (`PersonalPage-Binding-SelectedOptions.html`):

The **Model** will be as follows:

```
var person = {
  children: ["Jonnie", "Jane", "Richard", "Mary"],
  selectedChildren: ["Jonnie", "Mary"]
};
```

The **ViewModel** will be as follows:

```
var PersonViewModel = function() {
  var self = this;
  self.children = person.children;
  self.selectedChildren = person.selectedChildren
};
```

The **View** will be as follows:

```
<form>
  <select multiple="multiple" data-bind="options: children,
    selectedOptions: selectedChildren"></select>
</form>
```

The `selectedChildren` property of the ViewModel defines a set of selected items in the `select` element. Note that, as shown in the previous example, `selectedChildren` is a non-observable array; the preceding code only shows the use of the `selectedOptions` binding. In a real-world application, most of the time, the value of the `selectedChildren` binding will be an observable array.

Control flow bindings

The control flow bindings are a special kind of bindings that affect a group of elements or other bindings instead of a single element. Also, control flow bindings support alternative syntaxes with comments such as the following (for example, changing parts marked with []):

```
<!-- ko [binding-name]: [binding-value] -->
  [markup]
<!-- /ko -->
```

Let's learn about these kinds of bindings through examples.

The foreach binding

The `foreach` binding allows you to write a single markup that applies to each element in a collection of objects. It is very useful way to render lists and tables. Let's consider the following example (`PersonalPage-Binding-Foreach1.html`):

The **Model** will be as follows:

```
var person = {
  children: [
    { firstName: "Jonnie", age: 3 },
    { firstName: "Jane", age: 5 },
    { firstName: "Richard", age: 7},
    { firstName: "Mary", age: 9}
  ]
};
```

The **ViewModel** will be as follows:

```
var PersonViewModel = function() {
  var self = this;
  self.children = person.children
};
```

The **View** will be as follows:

```
<table>
  <thead>
    <tr><th>First name</th><th>Age</th></tr>
  </thead>
  <tbody data-bind="foreach: children">
    <tr>
      <td data-bind="text: firstName"></td>
      <td data-bind="text: age"></td>
    </tr>
  </tbody>
</table>
```

The `tbody` element in the View contains the `foreach` binding to the `children` property. It means that the inner content of the `tbody` section will be duplicated for every element in the collection. Also, inner bindings will be individually applied to each element. Knockout.js will automatically change the scope inside `foreach` to the current item. This is very intuitive and allows you to keep the data bindings simple.

Also, the foreach binding (as well as other control flow bindings) support an alternative syntax (PersonalPage-Binding-Foreach2.html):

```html
<table>
  <thead>
    <tr><th>First name</th><th>Age</th></tr>
  </thead>
  <tbody>
    <!-- ko foreach: children -->
    <tr>
      <td data-bind="text: firstName"></td>
      <td data-bind="text: age"></td>
    </tr>
    <!-- /ko -->
  </tbody>
</table>
```

 The foreach binding includes a huge number of advanced features; you can find the full list in the official documentation at http://knockoutjs.com/documentation/foreach-binding.html.

The if and ifnot bindings

The if binding is very similar to the visible binding, but there are two important differences:

1. The visible binding always keeps the contained markup in the DOM, unlike the if binding.

2. You can use the if binding even without a container element as shown in this example (PersonalPage-Binding-If.html). This can have performance implications. For small things that frequently change, it's best to use a visible binding to limit the DOM changes. For large chunks of HTML or things that don't change frequently, you can use the if binding.

The **View** will be as follows:

```html
<form>
  <input type="checkbox" data-bind="checked: showAbout" />
  Show about
</form>
```

```
<!-- ko if: showAbout-->
John's favorite site is <a href='http://www.packtpub.com'>PacktPub</
a>.
<!-- /ko -->
```

The `ifnot` binding works in exactly the opposite way. Consider the following line:

```
<!-- ko if: showAbout-->
```

You can replace the preceding line with the following:

```
<!-- ko ifnot: !showAbout() -->
```

 You can find additional information about the `if` and `ifnot` bindings in the documentation available at `http://knockoutjs.com/documentation/if-binding.html`.

The with binding

In previous examples, we always bind properties of HTML elements to properties of the ViewModel object. The `with` binding allows us to tell the container element (for example, `div`) that his descendant elements will bind to the properties of a specified object, not to the general ViewModel object. It can be very useful for a big ViewModel with a complex hierarchical structure. In other words, it allows you to change the scope of the ViewModel. Let's look at the `with` binding in the following example (`PersonalPage-Binding-With1.html`):

The **Model** will be as follows:

```
var person = {
  wife: {
    firstName: "Jessica",
    lastName: "Doe"
  }
};
```

The **ViewModel** will be as follows:

```
var PersonViewModel = function() {
  var self = this;
  self.wife = ko.observable(person.wife)
};
```

The **View** will be as follows:

```
<div data-bind="with: wife">
  Wife's first name: <span data-bind="text: firstName"></span>.<br
    />
  Wife's last name: <span data-bind="text: lastName"></span>.
</div>
```

The internal `span` elements bind to the properties of `wife` because they are placed inside the container with the `with: wife` data binding. Of course, the `with` binding also supports an alternative syntax (`PersonalPage-Binding-With2.html`). When the value of the `with` binding is not defined, the inner HTML of the binded element will not be rendered.

The **View** will be as follows:

```
<!-- ko with: wife -->
Wife's first name: <span data-bind="text: firstName"></span>.<br
  />
Wife's last name: <span data-bind="text: lastName"></span>.
<!-- /ko -->
```

 More information about the `with` binding can be found in the documentation available at `http://knockoutjs.com/documentation/with-binding.html`.

Computed observables

In this section, we will discuss a special way to create complex properties that depend on our existing observable properties. The standard approach in the Knockout.js library is **computed observables**. We will consider these kinds of properties with a simple example.

Using a computed observable

Let's add two base observable properties in the Model (the `person` object) and ViewModel (the `personViewModel` object): `firstName` and `lastName` (`PersonalPage-Computed1.html`). The initial values of these properties will be `John` and `Doe`, respectively.

...ill be as follows:

```
...son = {
    ...lame: "John",
    ...me: "Doe"
```

...del will be as follows:

```
var personViewModel = function() {
  var self = this;
  self.firstName = ko.observable(person.firstName);
  self.lastName = ko.observable(person.lastName);
};
```

The **View** will be as follows:

```
The first name: <span data-bind="text: firstName"></span><br />
The last name: <span data-bind="text: lastName"></span><br />
```

However, what if we want to work with the full name of a person as a single entity? The computed observables would help us.

Computed observables are special calculated properties. They depend on one or more other observables, and will automatically update after any dependencies change.

> Computed observable properties are a very powerful feature of Knockout.js that allow you to easily add application-UI specific logic to your website.

Let's create a computed observable for the full name (`PersonalPage-Computed2.html`):

The **ViewModel** will be as follows:

```
var personViewModel = function() {
  var self = this;
  self.firstName = ko.observable(person.firstName);
  self.lastName = ko.observable(person.lastName);
  self.fullName = ko.computed(function() {
    return self.firstName() + " " + self.lastName();
  })
};
```

The **View** will be as follows:

```
The name: <span data-bind="text: fullName"></span>
```

The `fullName` computed observable in the preceding code is defined with the `ko.observable` function by passing a function that presents how to calculate the desired value. The `fullName` observable depends on the `firstName` and `lastName` objects; any changes to the dependent properties will automatically update the `fullName` value.

Computed observable features

We will not consider computed observables in detail in this chapter because, usually, you don't need their advanced features for small and simple applications. This topic is beyond the scope of this book. However, it will be very useful to take a quick look at some of these features to gain knowledge of their existence. If you need these features in an application, you can always read about them in more detail in the official documentation. Some of the advanced computed observable features are as follows:

- **Dependency chains**: You can build a chain of properties that are dependent on each other. In the example in the previous section, the `fullName` property depends on the `firstName` and `lastName` properties. So, you can create the `aboutInformation` property that depends on the `fullName` property and some additional observables (for example, the `age` property, the `isMarried` property, and so on). Once `firstName` is updated, the dependency chain (including the `fullName` and `aboutInformation`) will also be updated.

- **Computed observables extenders**: In *Chapter 1, Introduction to Knockout.js*, we used the `extend` function to add additional behavior aspects to the observable property. Computed observables support extenders in the same way. For example, you can use `self.fullName.extend({notify: 'always'})` and `self.fullName.extend({rareLimit: 100})` to update `fullName` in a forced way and limit its change notifications.

- **Writeable computed observables**: Commonly, the computed observable is a read-only property because it supports only the read method. However, you can define your own custom logic to write a value to a property, for example, the following:

```
self.fullName = ko.computed({
  read: function () {
    return self.firstName() + " " + self.lastName();
  },
```

```
write: function (value) {
    var lastSpacePos = value.lastIndexOf(" ");
    if (lastSpacePos > 0) { // Ignore values with no space
character
        self.firstName(value.substring(0, lastSpacePos)); // Update
"firstName"
        self.lastName(value.substring(lastSpacePos + 1)); // Update
"lastName"
    }
},
owner: self
});
```

In this case, we will call it a **writeable property**.

> You can find much more information about computed observables in the official documentation available at `http://knockoutjs.com/documentation/computedObservables.html`.

Observable arrays

Usual observables allow us to create some property for which Knockout.js detects any changes. However, what if we want to work with a collection of objects and detect add and remove operations? The Knockout.js solution is **observable arrays**. We can use this special kind of arrays with the help of `ko.observableArray`. In this section, we will discuss how to use it in general, how to add new elements in an observable array, how to remove elements, and some useful manipulation functions for observable arrays.

Using an observable array

Very often, the real ViewModel objects contain collections of some elements. In this section, we will consider a very simple example with a collection in the ViewModel to demonstrate observable array usage. Let's add the `children` array for `person`, as shown in the following code (`PersonalPage-Arrays1.html`).

The **Model** will be as follows:

```
var person = {
    children: ["Jonnie", "Jane", "Richard", "Mary"]
};
```

The **ViewModel** will be as follows:

```
var personViewModel = function() {
  var self = this;
  self.children = ko.observableArray(person.children);
};
```

The **View** will be as follows:

```
<form>
  <select multiple="multiple" data-bind="options:
    children"></select>
</form>
```

In this example, the Model is replenished with a string array property, which is called `children`. The ViewModel also contains the `children` property, which is represented by an observable array. The View contains a very simple form with a `select` element. The `options` property of the element binds to the `children` property of the ViewModel.

Any add or remove operation with an observable array will automatically update the `select` element. The one important thing is that an observable array tracks the objects *in* the array, *not* the state of those objects. So, if you create an observable array from objects, it doesn't mean that these objects will also be observables.

Adding to an observable array

Let's update our example by adding operations with the created observable array (`PersonalPage-Arrays2.html`):

The **ViewModel** will be as follows:

```
var personViewModel = function() {
  var self = this;
  self.children = ko.observableArray(person.children);
  self.newChild = ko.observable("");
  self.addChildEnabled = ko.computed(function() {
    return self.newChild().length > 0;
  });
  self.addChild = function() {
    if (self.addChildEnabled()) {
      self.children.push(self.newChild());
      self.newChild("");
    }
  };
};
```

goes to observable

The **View** will be as follows:

```
<form data-bind="submit: addChild">
  New Child:
  <input data-bind='value: newChild, valueUpdate: "afterkeydown"'
    />
  <button type="submit" data-bind="enable: addChildEnabled"
    >Add</button>
  <p>Person's children:</p>
  <select multiple="multiple" size="7" data-bind="options:
    children"></select>
</form>
```

Let's look at this example line by line. We added the following things in the ViewModel:

- newChild: This is a string observable object to hold the name of a new child.
- canAddChild: This is a computed observable; it checks whether newChild is empty and returns true or false (we can't add a child with an empty name).
- addChild: This is a function to add a new child; it checks canAddChild and pushes a new child to the children array in the success case (newChild will be cleared after the child is added).

New things in the View are as follows:

- The input element for a new child name: its value property binds to newChild with the afterkeydown modifier
- The submit button element to add a new child (the submit event of the form binds to addChild): its enable property binds to canAddChild

You can run this example and check it. Try to add a new child via an interface. You will see an update of the select element with the children list.

Removing from an observable array

For deeper understanding of an observable array, we will see one more example. Let's upgrade our sample with multiple select remove operations (PersonalPage-Arrays3.html).

The **ViewModel** will be as follows:

```
var PersonViewModel = function() {
  var self = this;
  self.children = ko.observableArray(person.children);
```

```
self.selectedChildren = ko.observable([]);
self.newChild = ko.observable("");
self.addChildEnabled = ko.computed(function() {
  return self.newChild().length > 0;
});
self.addChild = function() {
  if (self.addChildEnabled()) {
    self.children.push(self.newChild());
    self.newChild("");
  }
};
self.removeSelectedEnabled = ko.computed(function() {
  return self.selectedChildren().length > 0;
});
self.removeSelected = function() {
  self.children.removeAll(self.selectedChildren());
  self.selectedChildren([]);
}
};
```

The **View** will be as follows:

```
<form data-bind="submit: addChild">
  New Child:
  <input data-bind='value: newChild, valueUpdate: "afterkeydown"'
    />
  <button type="submit" data-bind="enable: addChildEnabled">
    Add</button>
  <p>Person's children:</p>
  <select multiple="multiple" size="7" data-bind="options:
    children, selectedOptions: selectedChildren"></select><br />
  <button data-bind="click: removeSelected, enable:
    removeSelectedEnabled">Remove</button>
</form>
```

New things in the ViewModel are as follows:

- `selectedChildren`: This is an observable property to hold a set of selected items in the list.

- `removeSelectedEnabled`: This is a computed observable; it checks that the selection set is not empty and we can remove something.

- `removeSelected`: This is a function to remove the selected items.

New things in the View are as follows:

- The `select` element has additional bindings: `selectedOptions` binds to the `selectedChildren` property of the ViewModel.

- The `new` button element to remove the selected children. It has two bindings: `click` to `removeSelected` and `enable` to `removeSelectedEnabled`.

Now, we have a rich application that supports add and remove operations, which are implemented with the help of data bindings. Of course, this is just an example and applications have some limitations (for example, we will have troubles with namesakes and their removal), but it shows us how to work with observable arrays in the MVVM style. Button click events bind to the functions of the ViewModel and the `select` option binds to arrays. We did not write additional code to update the children list in the View after changes in the array, the Knockout.js tracking system did the job for us.

Manipulating an observable array

During the application development process, you will probably need some common operations for your collection, such as adding or removing elements, collection sorting, and so on. There are some functions to manipulate observable arrays:

- `push(value)`: This adds a value to the end of the array.

- `pop()`: This removes the last element from the array and returns it.

- `unshift(value)`: This inserts `value` at the beginning of the array.

- `shift()`: This removes the first element from the array and returns it.

- `reverse()`: This reverses the order of the array.

- `sort()`: This sorts the array of contents.

- `splice(start, count)`: This removes the `count` number of elements starting from `start`.

- `remove(value)`: This removes all elements that equal `value`.

- `remove(predicate)`: This removes all elements that satisfy the `predicate` function.

- `removeAll(set)`: This removes all elements that equal some element from `set`.

- `removeAll()`: This removes all values.

You can read a more detailed list in the official documentation available at `http://knockoutjs.com/documentation/observableArrays.html`.

Summary

In this section, we covered a huge number of useful Knockout.js features to build medium-size MVVM applications. We got acquainted with a set of standard bindings, including text and appearance bindings (`text`, `html`, `css`, `style`, `attr`, and `visible`), form field bindings (`value`, `click`, `submit`, `event`, `checked`, `enabled`, `disabled`, `options`, and `selectedOptions`), and control flow bindings (`foreach`, `if`, `ifnot`, and `with`). Also, we considered special kinds of observable properties, which very often come in handy during development: computed observables and observable arrays.

In the next chapter, we will apply this acquired knowledge to the ASP.NET site. We will look at how to integrate the Knockout.js library in an application and how to link client JavaScript and server C# logic.

3
Integrating Knockout.js in ASP.NET MVC Applications

In this chapter, we'll use our Knockout.js experience to create a simple ASP.NET MVC application. We'll create an application in pure Knockout.js plus ASP.NET MVC without external libraries. You'll also learn how to create a Model in C# and connect it with the MVVM structure in JavaScript.

We assume that you have some basic experience of developing ASP.NET MVC applications with Visual Studio, including familiarity with the Razor view engine. Also, we assume that you have got an understanding of the previous chapter, which explains the Knockout.js basics.

The list of topics that will be covered in this chapter are as follows:

- Creating an empty ASP.NET MVC application with Knockout.js support via NuGet
- Creating a C# Model and connecting it with JavaScript code
- Client-server interaction in a Knockout.js ASP.NET MVC application with the Razor view engine

Creating an application without Knockout.js

In this section, we will create a very simple ASP.NET MVC application with step by step instructions. We will use Visual Studio Express 2013 with Update 3 for Web (you can download for free it from the official site, http://www.visualstudio.com/), .NET Framework 4.5, and ASP.NET MVC 4 for this purpose, but you can use older or newer versions; the difference will be small.

The minimum requirements for this chapter are Visual Studio 2010, .NET Framework 4.0, and ASP.NET MVC 3.

Let's develop an application to store information about the home library. The application will allow users to manage their book lists, including standard **Create-Read-Update-Delete (CRUD)** operations (see http://en.wikipedia. org/wiki/Create,_read,_update_and_delete for more information). It should be noted that we will develop a study application; it shouldn't be considered a production-ready code. You will not find any interactions with a database, error handling, data validation, and other important aspects of a real application here. The source code will be written in a minimalist style because we need this example only for future work and to understand some key Knockout.js features. You can find the final version of the development solution in the HomeLibrary folder.

Creating a new project

In this section, you will learn how to create a new project in Visual Studio 2013. First of all, you should perform the following preparatory steps:

1. Launch the Visual Studio 2013 IDE.

2. Create a new **ASP.NET MVC 4 Web Application** project (go to the **File** menu and select **New | Project...**). Let's call the solution HomeLibrary and the project HomeLibrary1.

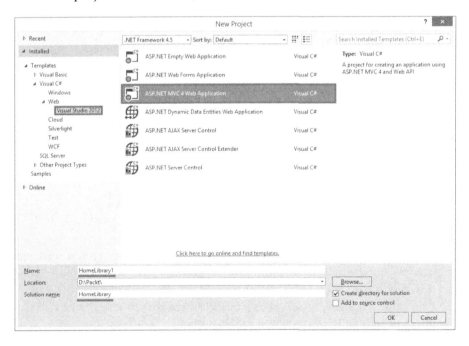

3. Select the **Basic** project template.

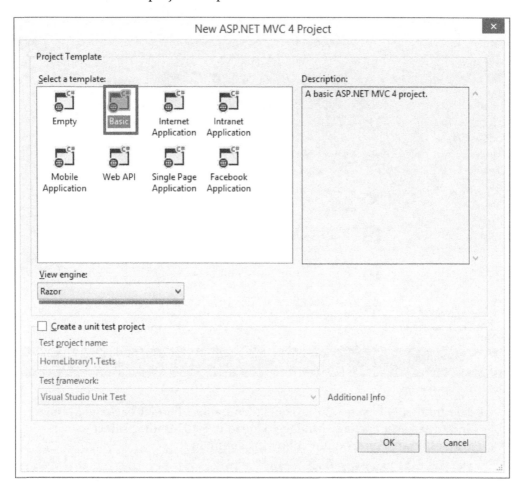

4. We don't want to work with the design of our pages in this example. Therefore, we will use the Bootstrap framework to make our site look nice. Bootstrap (http://getbootstrap.com/) is the popular HTML, CSS, and JS framework used to develop beautiful designs for web projects from ready components and blocks (or using ready CSS styles). We can install it via NuGet. NuGet (http://www.nuget.org/) is the package manager that will help us to add new dependencies with ease. There are two ways to install a library via NuGet.

Right-click on the project in **Solution Explorer**, select **Manage NuGet Packages…**, search for **Bootstrap**, and click on **Install**.

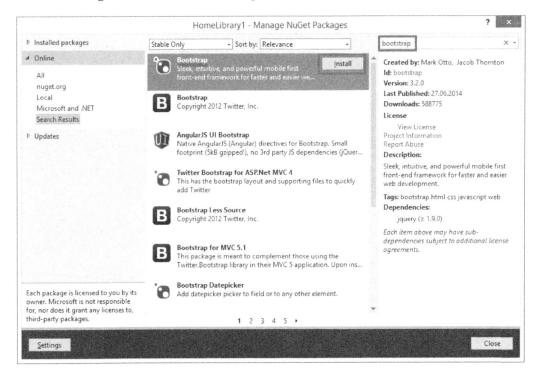

The another way is go to the **Tools** menu, select **NuGet Package Manager**, and then select **Package Manager Console**. Set **Default project** to **HomeLibrary1** and run the following command:

```
PM> Install-Package bootstrap
```

This is shown in the following screenshot:

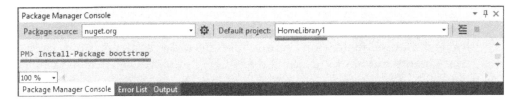

5. Open the `Views/Shared/_Layout.cshtml` file (it is the file that contains the default layout logic for your web pages) and add links to the Bootstrap library in the head section:

```
@Styles.Render("~/Content/bootstrap.css")
@Scripts.Render("~/Scripts/bootstrap.js")
```

Now we are ready to add some logic to our project.

Adding models

We will create two models: one for the book and one for the library. Go to **Solution Explorer**, right-click on the **Models** folder of your project, and select **Add | Class....** Let's call it `BookModel`. The source code is as follows:

```
namespace HomeLibrary1.Models
{
  public class BookModel
  {
    public int Id { get; set; }
    public string Title { get; set; }
    public string Author { get; set; }
    public int Year { get; set; }
  }
}
```

It is a really simple class. It contains four properties:

- `Id`: This is the identification number of the book
- `Title`: This is the title of the book
- `Author`: This is the author of the book
- `Year`: This is the publication year of the book

The second model will be called `LibraryModel` (you should create a corresponding file, as in the first case). The source code is as follows:

```
using System.Collections.Generic;

namespace HomeLibrary1.Models
{
  public class LibraryModel
  {
```

```
private readonly List<BookModel> books = new List
  <BookModel>();

private int nextId = 1;

public string Name { get; set; }

public LibraryModel()
{
  Name = "My home library";
  AddBook(new BookModel { Title = "Oliver Twist", Author =
    "Charles Dickens", Year = 1837 });
  AddBook(new BookModel { Title = "Winnie-the-Pooh", Author =
    "A. A. Milne", Year = 1926 });
  AddBook(new BookModel { Title = "The Hobbit", Author = "J.
    R. R. Tolkien", Year = 1937 });
  AddBook(new BookModel { Title = "The Bicentennial Man",
    Author = "Isaac Asimov", Year = 1976 });
  AddBook(new BookModel { Title = "The Green Mile", Author =
    "Stephen King", Year = 1996 });
}

public IEnumerable<BookModel> GetBooks()
{
  return books;
}

public BookModel GetBook(int id)
{
  return books.Find(b => b.Id == id);
}

public void AddBook(BookModel book)
{
  book.Id = nextId++;
  books.Add(book);
}

public bool UpdateBook(BookModel book)
{
  var index = books.FindIndex(b => b.Id == book.Id);
  if (index == -1)
    return false;
```

```
      books.RemoveAt(index);
      books.Insert(index, book);
      return true;
    }

  public void RemoveBook(int id)
  {
    books.RemoveAll(b => b.Id == id);
  }
  }
}
```

Let's examine the contents of this class:

- `books`: This is the private data of the class, which is the collection of all books in the library

- `nextId`: This is the identification number that will be used for the books that will be added in the library

- `Name`: This is the name of the library

- `LibraryModel`: In this constructor, we fill data (`Name` and `books`) with the initial values for demonstration purposes

- `GetBooks`: This gets all the books in the library

- `GetBook(int id)`: This gets a book with a specific identification number, `id`

- `AddBook(BookModel book)`: This adds a new book in the library

- `UpdateBook(BookModel book)`: This updates book data (book matching is performed by the identification number)

- `RemoveBook(int id)`: This removes a book with a specific identification number, `id`

Adding views

Now, we will create two views: one for the library overview (`Index`) and one to edit the information about a specific book (`Edit`).

1. First of all, let's create the `Library` subfolder (it will be the name of our controller) in the `Views` folder.

2. Next, right-click on the `Library` folder and click on **Add | View....**

3. Set **View name** to **Index**.

4. Set **View engine** to **Razor (CSHTML)**.

5. Check the **Create a strongly-typed view** checkbox.

6. Set **Model class** to **LibraryModel (HomeLibrary1.Models)**.

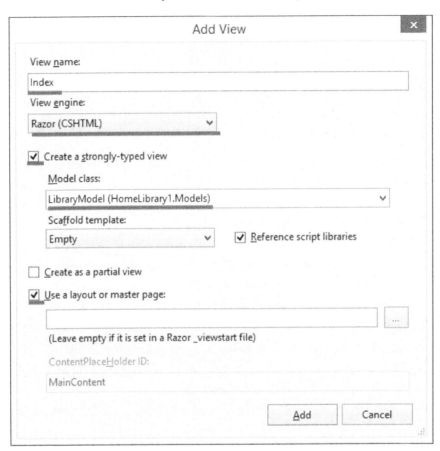

The source code is as follows:

```
@model HomeLibrary1.Models.LibraryModel
@{ ViewBag.Title = "Library"; }
<div class="container">
  <h2 style="text-align: center">@Model.Name</h2>
  <table class="table table-bordered table-striped table-condensed
    table-hover">
    <thead>
      <tr>
```

```
          <th>Title</th>
          <th>Author</th>
          <th>Year</th>
          <th>Actions</th>
        </tr>
      </thead>
      <tbody>
        @foreach (var book in Model.GetBooks())
        {
          <tr>
            <td>@book.Title</td>
            <td>@book.Author</td>
            <td>@book.Year</td>
            <td>
              @Html.ActionLink("Edit", "Edit", new { id = book.Id },
                new { @class = "btn btn-primary btn-xs" })
              @Html.ActionLink("Remove", "Remove", new { id = book.
                Id }, new { @class = "btn btn-primary btn-xs" })
            </td>
          </tr>
        }
      </tbody>
    </table>
    @Html.ActionLink("Add new book", "Add", null, new { @class =
      "btn btn-primary" })
</div>
```

Let's look at the code more carefully:

- The first line sets the type of model for the view (`LibraryModel`).

- The second line sets `ViewBag.Title` (this property is used in `_Layout.cshtml` to render the title element).

- The remaining lines describe the main layout of the page.

- The CSS classes (such as `container`, `table-striped`, `but-primary`, and so on) are described in the Bootstrap framework and are needed for pretty HTML rendering. You can just ignore them and focus on the substantive part of the code.

- The h2 element contains the name of the library (the `LibraryModel.Name` property).

- The list of books is represented as a table with four columns: three for the data (`Title`, `Author`, and `Year`) and one for the action button.

- We have two buttons per book: Edit and Remove (we will consider them in more detail with the controller discussion).

- Also, you can see the Add action button at the end of the page to add a new book.

We will also need another view for book editing. Let's call it **Edit**. You should add the corresponding class, as in the **Index** case, with one difference: **Model class** will be BookModel (HomeLibrary1.Models). The source code is as follows:

```
@model HomeLibrary1.Models.BookModel
@{ ViewBag.Title = "Edit book"; }
<div class="container">
  <h2 style="text-align: center">Edit book</h2>
  @using (Html.BeginForm("Edit", "Library", FormMethod.Post,
  new { @class = "form-horizontal", role = "form" }))
  {
    <div class="form-group">
      @Html.LabelFor(m => m.Title, new { @class = "col-sm-2
        control-label" })
      <div class="col-sm-10">
        @Html.TextBoxFor(m => m.Title, new { @class = "form-
          control" })
      </div>
    </div>
    <div class="form-group">
      @Html.LabelFor(m => m.Author, new { @class = "col-sm-2
        control-label" })
      <div class="col-sm-10">
        @Html.TextBoxFor(m => m.Author, new { @class = "form-
          control" })
      </div>
    </div>
    <div class="form-group">
      @Html.LabelFor(m => m.Year, new { @class = "col-sm-2
        control-label" })
      <div class="col-sm-10">
        @Html.TextBoxFor(m => m.Year, new { @class = "form-
          control" })
      </div>
    </div>
    <div class="form-group">
      <div class="col-sm-12">
```

```
        <input type="submit" class="btn btn-primary pull-right"
          value="Save" />
      </div>
    </div>
  }
</div>
```

It is a simple form with three fields: Title, Caption, and Year. You can see the Save button at the end of the form to save the results. The CSS classes were also taken from the Bootstrap framework.

Adding the Controller

It's time to create the Controller. It is the main class of our application because it is responsible for the main logic and interaction between models and views. Let's create a new Controller and call it LibraryController (right click on the **Controllers** folder of the project in **Solution Explorer** and select **Add | Controller...**). In our case, we need to select the **Empty MVC controller** template, as shown in the following screenshot:

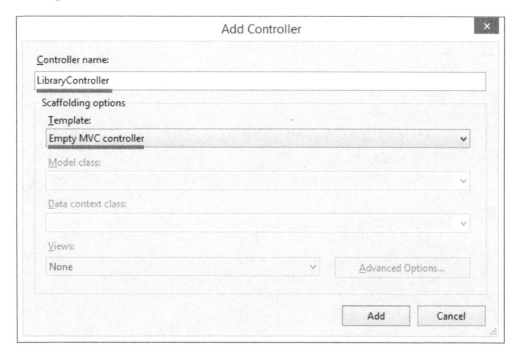

You should write the following code for the Controller:

```
using HomeLibrary1.Models;
using System;
using System.Web.Mvc;

namespace HomeLibrary1.Controllers
{
  public class LibraryController : Controller
  {
    private static readonly LibraryModel Library = new LibraryModel();

    public ActionResult Index()
    {
      return View(Library);
    }

    [HttpGet]
    public ActionResult Edit(int id)
    {
      return View(Library.GetBook(id));
    }

    [HttpPost]
    public ActionResult Edit(BookModel book)
    {
      Library.UpdateBook(book);
      return RedirectToAction("Index");
    }

    public ActionResult Add()
    {
      var book = new BookModel
      {
        Title = "New Book",
        Author = "Unknown",
        Year = DateTime.Now.Year
      };
```

```
        Library.AddBook(book);
        return RedirectToAction("Index");
    }

    public ActionResult Remove(int id)
    {
      Library.RemoveBook(id);
      return RedirectToAction("Index");
    }
  }
}
```

Let's discuss it in detail. `Library` is the main model of our library; it is a static field for demonstration purposes (in the real application, it will likely be a database or another external data source). The model methods are as follows:

- `Index()`: This method returns the `Index` view with our library overview logic

- `[HttpGet] Edit(int id)`: This method returns the `Edit` view to edit the book with the identification number `id`

- `[HttpPost] Edit(BookModel book)`: This methods takes the edited book's data, updates it in the library, and returns the `Index` view

- `Add()`: This method adds a book in the library and returns the `Index` view

- `Remove(int id)`: This method removes the book with the identification number `id` and return the `Index` view

Running the application

Only a final touch remains. Open the `App_start/RouteConfig.cs` file and update the line with the `defaults` parameters with the `Library` controller (see http:// msdn.microsoft.com/en-us/library/vstudio/cc668201(v=vs.100).aspx for more information):

```
defaults: new { controller = "Library", action = "Index", id =
  UrlParameter.Optional }
```

This means that our `LibraryController` will be the default controller when an application starts. Now, you can choose your favorite browser on the Visual Studio toolbar (see the following screenshot):

The work is finished! Just press *Ctrl + F5* and enjoy! You can see the result in the following screenshot.

The following is the main view:

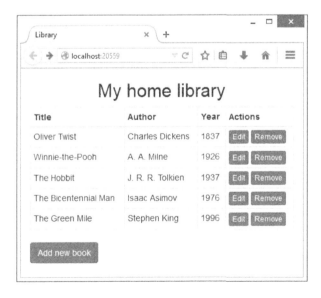

This is the edit view:

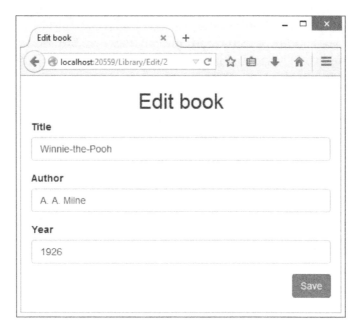

In this section, we obtained a complete working application that supports CRUD operations. Explore the source code and play with the rendered pages. In the next section, we will improve this example with the power of Knockout.js. You should be able to easily navigate through your code before moving on the next step.

Creating an application with Knockout.js

In this section, we will update a sample with Knockout.js from the previous section. For this purpose, we will create a new project with similar functionality and reprocessed source code. We will compare two samples (with and without Knockout.js) to understand how Knockout.js can help us develop a rich ASP.NET MVC application the easy way.

Motivation

The current state of our `HomeLibrary` project has one fatal drawback: Add and Delete actions entail a full page reload. This has a negative impact on the volume of traffic and the speed of query execution.

In the real application, it can be a serious problem. Just imagine: you have a very big page and the user wants to update only a small part of it. In this case, it will be very sad if you reload the full page. Modern applications should be responsive. They should take a small volume of traffic and immediately respond to user actions. This is particularly important in view of the increased number of mobile users, who have weak devices and slow, limited traffic.

The standard way in this case is **Asynchronous JavaScript and XML (AJAX)**. It is a group of techniques that help you perform a background request to the server and use the response to update only one part of the page. However, implementing the fully updated logic manually on pure JavaScript is routine activity.

Fortunately, we can use Knockout.js to dynamically update the target part of the page according to declarative bindings.

Creating a new project

Let's create a new project in our solution from the previous section and call it `HomeLibrary2`. It also will be an ASP.NET MVC4 application that is based on the Basic template. We need the following libraries: `bootstrap`, `knockoutjs`, and `jQuery`. You can install these libraries from **Package Manager Console** using the following commands with `HomeLibrary2` as a default project:

```
PM> Install-Package bootstrap
PM> Install-Package knockoutjs
PM> Install-Package jQuery
```

If you already have some of these libraries in the project template, the given command will update it to the latest version. In this book, we will work with `bootstrap 3.2.0`, `knockoutjs 3.1.0`, and `jQuery 2.1.1`, but you can work with other versions of these libraries, as well. Let's add a link to the libraries in the head section of the `Views/Shared/_Layout.cshtml` file:

```
@Styles.Render("~/Content/bootstrap.css")
@Scripts.Render("~/Scripts/bootstrap.js")
@Scripts.Render("~/Scripts/knockout-3.1.0.js")
@Scripts.Render("~/Scripts/jquery-2.1.1.js")
```

Adding models

We will use the same model as in the previous section. You can just copy the code of the `BookModel` and `LibraryModel` classes to a new project. Just do not forget to change the namespace to `HomeLibrary2`.

Adding views

The Edit view will be taken from HomeLibrary1. We will use the Index view to demonstrate applying the Knockout.js approach for our application. Let's implement the following source code for the Index view:

```
@model HomeLibrary2.Models.LibraryModel
@{ ViewBag.Title = "HomeLibrary"; }
<div class="container">
  <h2 style="text-align: center"><span data-bind="text:
    Name"></span></h2>
  <table class="table table-bordered table-striped table-condensed
    table-hover">
    <thead>
      <tr>
        <th>Title</th>
        <th>Author</th>
        <th>Year</th>
        <th>Actions</th>
      </tr>
    </thead>
    <tbody data-bind="foreach: Books">
      <tr>
        <td data-bind="text: Title"></td>
        <td data-bind="text: Author"></td>
        <td data-bind="text: Year"></td>
        <td>
          <a href="#" data-bind="click: $root.edit" class="btn
            btn-primary btn-xs">Edit</a>
          <a href="#" data-bind="click: $root.remove" class="btn
            btn-primary btn-xs">Remove</a>
        </td>
      </tr>
    </tbody>
  </table>
  <a href="#" data-bind="click: add" class="btn btn-primary">Add
    new book</a>
</div>

<script type="text/javascript">
  var libraryViewModel = function () {
    var self = this;
    self.Name = ko.observable();
    self.Books = ko.observableArray();

    // Initial data
    $.ajax({
      url: '@Url.Action("GetName")',
```

```
    cache: false,
    type: 'GET',
    contentType: 'application/json; charset=utf-8',
    data: {},
    success: function (data) {
      self.Name(data);
    }
  });
  $.ajax({
    url: '@Url.Action("GetBooks")',
    cache: false,
    type: 'GET',
    contentType: 'application/json; charset=utf-8',
    data: {},
    success: function (data) {
      self.Books(data);
    }
  });

  // Remove
  self.remove = function (book) {
    var id = book.Id;
    $.ajax({
      url: '@Url.Action("Remove")',
      cache: false,
      type: 'POST',
      contentType: 'application/json; charset=utf-8',
      data: JSON.stringify({ id: id }),
      dataType: "json",
      success: function (data) {
        self.Books(data);
      }
    });
  }

  // Add
  self.add = function () {
    $.ajax({
      url: '@Url.Action("Add")',
      cache: false,
      type: 'GET',
      contentType: 'application/json; charset=utf-8',
      data: {},
      success: function (data) {
        self.Books(data);
      }
    });
  }
```

```
    // Edit
    self.edit = function (book) {
      var id = book.Id;
      location.href = "Library/Edit/" + id;
    }
  }
  // Applying bindings
  ko.applyBindings(new libraryViewModel());
</script>
```

There are some distinctions from the previous version of the view. The first distinction is migrating to Knockout.js. Indeed, we use the `foreach` binding instead of Razor `@foreach` for enumeration of books, `text` binding instead of Razor rendering methods for the main data (`Name` for our library and `Title`, `Author`, and `Year` for its books), and `click` binding instead of Razor `@Html.ActionLink` for actions.

Also, we define a large amount of JavaScript source code. In the code, you can see the creation of a `ViewModel` to store the server `LibraryModel` data (it is called `libraryViewModel`) and apply it using the `ko.applyBindings(new libraryViewModel())` statement. Let's discuss the declaration of `libraryViewModel` in detail. This declaration starts with the following lines:

```
var self = this;
self.Name = ko.observable();
self.Books = ko.observableArray();
```

The first line is our usual technique to work with `this` via its local alias `self`. The second and third lines define observable properties of ViewModel: `Name` and `Books`. These properties correspond to original properties of the server `LibraryModel` class.

After that, we start to load data from the server with the following code:

```
$.ajax({
  url: '@Url.Action("GetName")',
  cache: false,
  type: 'GET',
  contentType: 'application/json; charset=utf-8',
  data: {},
  success: function (data) {
    self.Name(data);
  }
});
```

The preceding code describes the AJAX request to the server. `$` is the main jQuery object, `$.ajax` is a special method to perform the AJAX request the easy way. This method works with the following properties:

- `url`: This is the URL address for the request; we define it via Razor `@Url.Action`

- `cache`: For this, a `false` value will force the requested page to not be cached by the browser

- `type`: In this case, we perform the GET request to get some data from the server

- `contentType`: In this case, we want to get data in the JSON format with the UTF-8 charset

- `data`: This is the data that transforms to the server; it is empty in this case

- `success`: This is the callback function for the success case; after performing a request, we should update the `Name` property of the `ViewModel`

Likewise, we load the list of books. We also declare three methods for the `ViewModel`: `remove`, `add`, and `edit`.

The logic of the `add` method is very similar to the logic of loading books, but with one distinction: we change the parameters of `url` to `@Url.Action("Add")`. The `Add` server methods add a new book and return the full book list in the JSON format.

The logic of the `remove` method is also similar to the logic of loading books, but it has more distinctions. In addition to changing the parameters of `url` (to `@Url.Action("Remove")`), this method should transform the identification number `id` of the deleted book to the server. It means that we should change the request type from GET to POST and set the `data` parameter to `JSON.stringify({ id: id })` (it is a special way to form the `id` value in the right JSON format).

The `edit` method is very simple. In this case, we don't need to perform any AJAX request, we just change `location.href` of the page to the editing page (the `Edit` view) of the book with the given identification number `id`.

Adding the controller

In this section, we will write a controller that will contain the main application logic and discuss this logic in detail. Let's implement a new logic for our Controller:

```
using System;
using System.Web.Mvc;
```

```csharp
using HomeLibrary2.Models;

namespace HomeLibrary2.Controllers
{
  public class LibraryController : Controller
  {
    private static readonly LibraryModel Library = new
      LibraryModel();

    public ActionResult Index()
    {
      return View(Library);
    }

    public JsonResult GetName()
    {
      return Json(Library.Name, JsonRequestBehavior.AllowGet);
    }

    public JsonResult GetBooks()
    {
      return Json(Library.GetBooks(),
        JsonRequestBehavior.AllowGet);
    }
    [HttpGet]
    public ActionResult Edit(int id)
    {
      return View(Library.GetBook(id));
    }


    [HttpPost]
    public ActionResult Edit(BookModel book)
    {
      Library.UpdateBook(book);
      return RedirectToAction("Index");
    }

    public JsonResult Add()
    {
      var book = new BookModel
        {
```

```
      Title = "New book",
      Author = "Unknown",
      Year = DateTime.Now.Year
    };
    Library.AddBook(book);
    return Json(Library.GetBooks(),
      JsonRequestBehavior.AllowGet);
  }

  public JsonResult Remove(int id)
  {
    Library.RemoveBook(id);
    return Json(Library.GetBooks(),
      JsonRequestBehavior.AllowGet);
  }
  }
}
```

This code is very similar to the LibraryController from HomeLibrary1, but it has some important distinctions:

- The Add and Remove methods return JsonResult instead of ActionResult. This means that they return only the target data in the JSON format instead of the full HTML page. In this case, the target data is the book list of the library. The JSON data is returned with the following code:

```
return Json(Library.GetBooks(),
  JsonRequestBehavior.AllowGet);
```

- The model has two additional methods: GetName and GetBooks. These methods are used for the initial data loading and also to return values in the JSON format.

Running the application

Set the default controller (in the same way as we did in HomeLibrary1) and run the application. The external behavior is identical to the previous project, but inside there were some changes. Open your favorite tool for network analysis (for example, the internal tool in the Firefox browser) and remove some books. You will see a new request to the server (Remove).

Check that the response contains only the book list instead of the full page (see the following screenshot):

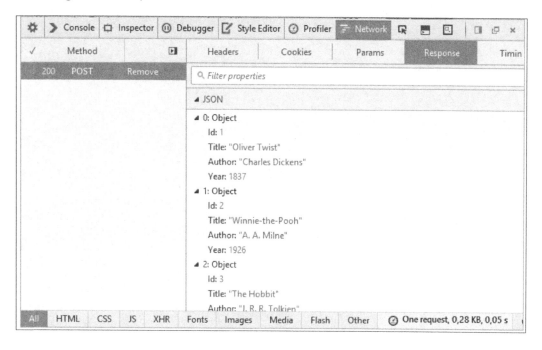

Summary

In this chapter, we started with a very simple ASP.NET MVC application to store information about the home library. The first version of the application (HomeLibrary1) was developed in pure ASP.NET MVC without additional JavaScript code. After that, we updated the internal logic with the Knockout.js library (HomeLibrary2). Thanks to the AJAX request, we were able to interact with the user without regular full page reloads. This approach reduces traffic, improves the performance, and makes the design more responsive. Knockout.js provides us with an easy way to create a view with declarative bindings. We shouldn't worry about writing JavaScript code for UI update; Knockout.js would take care of this for us.

In the next chapter, we will update the acquired application with the Knockout MVC library. We will learn how Knockout MVC can help us to simplify the development of applications based on Knockout.js.

4
Creating a Web Application with Knockout MVC

Knockout MVC is an ASP.NET library for using Knockout.js. With this library, you can create a powerful web application based on Knockout.js data bindings without any line of JavaScript code.

In this chapter, we'll be discussing how to move an entire business logic to the server side; the complete necessary JavaScript code on the client side will be generated automatically based on the described C# (or VB.NET) model.

The list of topics that will be covered in this chapter are as follows:

- An overview of Knockout MVC and the motivation for its use
- When you should use Knockout MVC, and when you should not
- Getting started with Knockout MVC and developing a "Hello World" application
- Basic aspects of Knockout MVC
- How to create a simple CRUD Knockout MVC application

Getting started with Knockout MVC

In this section, we will take a look at Knockout MVC, including a brief introduction, the motivation for using it, an installation guide, and useful links.

Knockout MVC is a library for ASP.NET MVC, which is a wrapper for Knockout.js. It can be useful if you want to move all of your business logic to the server side, as it allows you to avoid duplication of the server data model on the client side. You can develop a client-server application without writing a single line of JavaScript code. The interaction between the view and model is described in the familiar MVVM style. You also don't need JavaScript for it because you can use C# expressions for this purpose (you can also use VB.NET instead of C#).

The Knockout MVC library performs the transformation of your business model from C# to JavaScript. It also generates all the JavaScript logic needed to implement the interaction between a client and server, and turns your C# binding expressions into JavaScript analogues. The generated JavaScript code is based on Knockout. js, so it will have all of the Knockout.js benefits, such as high working speed and compatibility with mainstream browsers.

Motivation

If you develop a client-server web application on pure ASP.NET MVC without any additional libraries, you should ideally implement the following parts in a general case:

- A data model on the client side (JavaScript)
- A data model on the server side (C#)
- Logic for initialization of fields on the client side: (JavaScript)
- Logic for data model processing on the client side (JavaScript)
- Logic for data serialization and its transmission to the server on the client side (JavaScript)
- Logic for receiving data from the client and its deserialization on the server side (C#)
- Logic for data processing on the server side (C#)
- Logic for data serialization and its transmission to the client on the server side (C#)
- Logic for receiving data from the server and its deserialization on the client side (JavaScript)
- Logic for updating an interface according to the new data on the client side (JavaScript)

Supporting such code can be a problem. You should make changes very carefully with full synchronization between the client (JavaScript) and server (C#) sides. An IDE can't help you with refactoring. Also, don't check any client-side typing issues in the compiling step.

The Knockout MVC library allows you to move all of your code to the server side. You can only use the C# language to describe a data model and processing logic. Declarative bindings for interface rendering will be based on C# expressions with IntelliSense and type checking support.

When you should use Knockout MVC

It is very important to understand when you should use Knockout MVC and when you shouldn't. The following items indicate when Knockout MVC can be useful for you:

- You need an easy way to create a client-server web application without writing JavaScript code
- You want syntax checking and type checking in the compilation stage
- All of your data processing methods should be performed on the server side

However, you should understand that Knockout MVC isn't a universal approach or a silver bullet to develop any kind of ASP.NET MVC applications, and you should pay for the library benefits. Its main drawback is that you send the entire ViewModel from the client to the server on any action (Knockout MVC supports partial models but this way is not always convenient to use). So, if you have a very big ViewModel, maybe you don't want to send all of the data to the server on each small request. The second drawback of Knockout MVC is the requirement to implement all of your logic on the server side. On the one hand, it's good because you can use C# to describe your logic. However, on the other hand, you should perform the request for any user action under the model. Of course, you can expand the main Knockout MVC logic with some native Knockout.js logic, but in this case, you lose the main Knockout MVC advantages, such as the absence of a need to synchronize the C# and the JavaScript logic.

So, you probably shouldn't use Knockout MVC in the following cases:

- You have a big model and you don't want to send the entire model on each request
- You want to implement a part of the logic only on the client side

You should weigh all of the pros and cons of each approach, and make a decision whether to use the Knockout MVC library or not before the development phase, according to the specification and business requirements of your project.

Installation

First of all, you should prepare your project to work with Knockout MVC. In this section, we will install the library, include additional JavaScript libraries, and create the main template. You should perform the following steps in order to be ready to use Knockout MVC:

1. Prepare an ASP.NET MVC project as we did in the previous chapter.

2. Install Knockout MVC from NuGet. You can search for the kMVC package via Visual Studio Package Manager or run the following line in the **Package Manager Console**:

   ```
   PM> Install-Package kMVC
   ```

3. Add links to the following libraries in the head section of your layout (the `Views/Shared/_Layout.cshtml` file for the standard templates). You should replace `x.y.z` with your specific versions of the jQuery and Knockout.js libraries:

   ```
   <script src="@Url.Content("~/Scripts/jquery-x.y.z.min.js")"
     type="text/javascript"></script>
   <script src="@Url.Content("~/Scripts/knockout-x.y.z.js")"
     type="text/javascript"></script>
   <script src="@Url.Content("~/Scripts/knockout.mapping-
     latest.js")" type="text/javascript"></script>
   <script src="@Url.Content("~/Scripts/
     perpetuum.knockout.js")" type="text/javascript"></script>
   ```

   The jQuery library is optional; you can skip this include line for a simple project, but some advanced Knockout MVC features use jQuery (for example, the AJAX API). The `knockout.mapping-latest` library helps us send our ViewModel between the client side and the server side. The `perpetuum.knockout` library contains some helpful functions to send the AJAX request to the server.

4. You can start with the following template for a View (we will consider the code in more detail shortly):

   ```
   @using PerpetuumSoft.Knockout
   @model <!-- You model -->
   @{
     var ko = Html.CreateKnockoutContext();
   }
   ```

```
<!-- Your page -->

@ko.Apply(Model)
```

In this basic template, `PerpetuumSoft` is the name of the root namespace of Perpetuum Software LLC projects. This company developed the Knockout MVC library.

5. Inherit your controller from `KnockoutController`, as shown in the following example:

```
public class FooController : KnockoutController {
  public ActionResult Index()
  {
    return View();
  }
}
```

That's all! Now you are ready to write the target logic for your application.

Useful links

You can find more useful information about Knockout MVC at the following links:

- Official site: `http://knockoutmvc.com/`
- Documentation: `http://knockoutmvc.com/Home/Documentation`
- Source code: `https://github.com/AndreyAkinshin/knockout-mvc`
- Forum: `https://groups.google.com/forum/#!forum/knockout-mvc`

Working with the Hello World example in Knockout MVC

Let's create an application based on a very simple model. It will contain only two properties: `FirstName` and `LastName`. The View will contain two `TextBox` elements to edit properties and a `span` element with a greeting text. You can find the full code of the example in the supplement code bundle of this book (`HomeLibrary/HelloWorld`) or look for the live example on the official site (`http://knockoutmvc.com/HelloWorld`).

Let's create a new ASP.NET MVC 4 project and install the kMVC packages via NuGet.

Adding the model

First of all, we should create a model. We will work with a very simple example. Let's define the following model (HelloWorld/Models/HelloWorldModel.cs):

```
using System.Web.Script.Serialization;
using DelegateDecompiler;
using Newtonsoft.Json;

namespace HelloWorld.Models
{
    public class HelloWorldModel
    {
        public string FirstName { get; set; }
        public string LastName { get; set; }

        [Computed]
        [ScriptIgnore]
        [JsonIgnore]
        public string FullName
        {
            get { return FirstName + " " + LastName; }
        }
    }
}
```

The HelloWorldModel class has two simple auto properties: FirstName and LastName. The FullName property is of particular interest. First of all, it has only the getter method that returns an expression. This expression will be transformed into a JavaScript expression, but we need more work for that. Note that the property has three attributes (and the behavior may change in future versions of the library). The Computed attribute from the DelegateDecompiler namespace means that Knockout MVC turns the property to the JavaScript method. The ScriptIgnore and JsonIgnore attributes mean that Knockout MVC shouldn't work with the property during serialization because the property is actually a method, not data.

Note that in this example we refer to two additional libraries: DelegateDecompiler and Newtonsoft.Json. The first one helps to decompile our expression and convert it to JavaScript. The second one helps us work with JSON. These libraries were installed during the kMVC package installation.

Adding the controller

Also, we need a controller. In this example, we will work with a very simple controller. It will contain a single `Index` method for the main view of our application. Let's define the following controller (`HelloWorld/Controllers/HelloWorldController`):

```
using System.Web.Mvc;
using HelloWorld.Models;
using PerpetuumSoft.Knockout;

namespace HelloWorld.Controllers
{
    public class HelloWorldController : KnockoutController
    {
        public ActionResult Index()
        {
            ViewBag.Title = "Hello world";
            return View(new HelloWorldModel
            {
                FirstName = "Steve",
                LastName = "Sanderson"
            });
        }
    }
}
```

The controller is inherited from `KnockoutController`. This provides us with overridden logic for JSON conversion operations. The `Index` method is very simple; it sets `ViewBag.Title` and returns `View` with a new `HelloWorldModel` (the initial value of the property is the name of the author of Knockout.js—Steve Sanderson).

Adding the view

The view will contain elements to display the `FirstName`, the `LastName`, and the `FullName`. Let's define the following view (`HelloWorld/Views/HelloWorld/Index.cshtml`):

```
@using PerpetuumSoft.Knockout
@model HelloWorld.Models.HelloWorldModel
@{ var ko = Html.CreateKnockoutContext(); }
```

```
<p>First name: @ko.Html.TextBox(m => m.FirstName)</p>
<p>Last name: @ko.Html.TextBox(m => m.LastName)</p>
<h2>Hello, @ko.Html.Span(m => m.FullName)!</h2>
@ko.Apply(Model)
```

The following is the most interesting part of this example. Let's discuss each line in detail.

- `@using PerpetuumSoft.Knockout`: We add the `PerpetuumSoft.Knockout` namespace; it makes the method for creating `KnockoutContext` available.

- `@model HelloWorld.Models.HelloWorldModel`: We set the model class for the page.

- `@{ var ko = Html.CreateKnockoutContext(); }`: We create the main Knockout MVC object, `KnockoutContext`, and call it `ko` (by analogy with the main Knockout.js object, which is also called `ko`). This object allows us to use all the Knockout MVC methods needed.

- `<p>First name: @ko.Html.TextBox(m => m.FirstName)</p>`: We use the `ko` object to define `TextBox` with a binding. To be more precise, we bind the `text` property of `TextBox` to the `FirstName` property of `HelloWorldModel`.

- `<p>Last name: @ko.Html.TextBox(m => m.LastName)</p>`: We create `TextBox` and bind its `text` property to the `LastName` property of the model, similar to the previous line.

- `<h2>Hello, @ko.Html.Span(m => m.FullName)!</h2>`: We create a `Span` element and bind its `text` property to the `FullName` property. Note that `FullName` is a computed property, but the syntax is exactly the same as in the case of usual properties.

- `@ko.Apply(Model)`: We apply binding to our model. This line renders the complete JavaScript code that works with the native Knockout.js library, and implements the target logic.

Don't forget to add links to the JavaScript libraries in the layout template (step 3 in the *Installation* section).

Running the application

Let's change the default controller (in the `HelloWorld/App_Start/RouteConfig.cs` file) to `HelloWorld` and run the application:

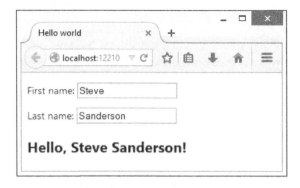

The "Hello" message depends on the values in TextBox elements. As soon as one of the values is changed, the message will be immediately updated.

Under the hood

For better understanding of the library, it will be useful to look at the generated source code:

```
<p>First name: <input data-bind="value : FirstName"
  name="FirstName" type="text" /></p>
<p>Last name: <input data-bind="value : LastName" name="LastName"
  type="text" /></p>
<h2>Hello, <span data-bind="text : FullName"></span>!</h2>

<script type="text/javascript">
  var viewModelJs = {"FirstName":"Steve","LastName":"Sanderson"};
  var viewModel = ko.mapping.fromJS(viewModelJs);
  viewModel.FullName = ko.computed(function() { try { return
    ((this.FirstName() + ' ') + this.LastName())} catch(e) {
    return null; }  ;}, viewModel);
  ko.applyBindings(viewModel);
</script>
```

You can see that the C# binding turns into JavaScript binding directly inside the HTML elements. The @ko.Apply(Model) was transformed in the Knockout.js initialization code. Let's discuss each line in detail.

- var viewModelJs = {"FirstName":"Steve","LastName":"Sanderson"};: This sets the initial values of the models in the JSON format.

- var viewModel = ko.mapping.fromJS(viewModelJs);: This transforms the initial data to the Knockout.js model with the help of the Knockout.mapping library.

- `viewModel.FullName = ko.computed(function() { try { return ((this.FirstName() + ' ') + this.LastName())} catch(e) { return null; } ;}, viewModel);`: This declares the computed observable function for the `FullName` calculation.

- `ko.applyBindings(viewModel);`: When you use Knockout.js directly, you should call the JavaScript `ko.applyBindings` method for your ViewModel. It applies binding to the view. This line is just a wrapper to apply native Knockout.js binding.

Developing a Knockout MVC application

In this section, we will take the `HomeLibrary` application from the previous chapter and update it with Knockout MVC. We will discuss how this approach can help us simplify an ASP.NET application and allow us to get rid of the client JavaScript code.

Adding the model

We will update the model from the `HomeLibrary2` project, as seen in *Chapter 3, Integrating Knockout.js in ASP.NET MVC Applications*. The `BookModel` class will "be equal to the version from the old project:

```
namespace HomeLibrary3.Models
{
  public class BookModel
  {
    public int Id { get; set; }
    public string Title { get; set; }
    public string Author { get; set; }
    public int Year { get; set; }
  }
}
```

The `LibraryModel` will be a little easier than its previous version:

```
using System.Collections.Generic;

namespace HomeLibrary3.Models
{
  public class LibraryModel
  {
    public List<BookModel> Books { get; set; }
    public int NextId { get; set; }
```

```
    public string Name { get; set; }

    public BookModel GetBook(int id)
    {
      return Books.Find(b => b.Id == id);
    }

    public void AddBook(BookModel book)
    {
      book.Id = NextId++;
      Books.Add(book);
    }

    public bool UpdateBook(BookModel book)
    {
      var index = Books.FindIndex(b => b.Id == book.Id);
      if (index == -1)
        return false;
      Books.RemoveAt(index);
      Books.Insert(index, book);
      return true;
    }
  }
}
```

Please note the following important updates:

- All data members of the model (Books, NextId, and Name) are public now. This allows you to serialize and deserialize the model.
- The GetBooks and RemoveBook methods were removed because now we can use the public Books property for the corresponding aims.
- The initialization logic was removed (we will see it later in the controller).

Adding the controller

There are some important changes to the controller. This includes the rewriting of the Add, Remove, and Edit methods. A detailed description of the changes is placed after the example:

```
using System;
using System.Collections.Generic;
using System.Web.Mvc;
using HomeLibrary3.Models;

namespace HomeLibrary3.Controllers
```

```
{
    public class LibraryController : Controller
    {
        private static LibraryModel Library;

        static LibraryController()
        {
            var model = new LibraryModel
            {
                Name = "My home library",
                Books = new List<BookModel>(),
                NextId = 1
            };
            model.AddBook(new BookModel { Title = "Oliver Twist",
                Author = "Charles Dickens", Year = 1837 });
            model.AddBook(new BookModel { Title = "Winnie-the-
                Pooh", Author = "A. A. Milne", Year = 1926 });
            model.AddBook(new BookModel { Title = "The Hobbit",
                Author = "J. R. R. Tolkien", Year = 1937 });
            model.AddBook(new BookModel { Title = "The
                Bicentennial Man", Author = "Isaac Asimov", Year =
                1976 });
            model.AddBook(new BookModel { Title = "The Green Mile"
                , Author = "Stephen King", Year = 1996 });
            Library = model;
        }

        public ActionResult Index()
        {
            return View(Library);
        }

        public ActionResult Edit(int index)
        {
            return View(Library.Books[index]);
        }

        [HttpPost]
        public ActionResult Edit(BookModel book)
        {
            Library.UpdateBook(book);
            return RedirectToAction("Index");
        }

        public ActionResult EditRedirect(LibraryModel
            clientLibrary, int index)
```

```
        {
            Library = clientLibrary;
            return Json(new { redirect = true, url = "Library/
              Edit?index=" + index });
        }

        public ActionResult Add(LibraryModel clientLibrary)
        {
            var book = new BookModel
            {
                Title = "New book",
                Author = "Unknown",
                Year = DateTime.Now.Year
            };
            clientLibrary.AddBook(book);
            Library = clientLibrary;
            return Json(clientLibrary);
        }

        public ActionResult Remove(LibraryModel clientLibrary, int
          index)
        {
            clientLibrary.Books.RemoveAt(index);
            Library = clientLibrary;
            return Json(clientLibrary);
        }
    }
}
```

Let's discuss some of the updates in detail.

- The initialization logic of the model is in the constructor of the controller.

- The GetBooks and the GetName methods were removed because now we can bind to the corresponding data directly via the model, with the help of Knockout MVC.

- The [HttpGet] Edit method turned into two methods: Edit and EditRedirect. The new Edit method just returns the Edit view for the target book by index. The EditRedirect method returns a special redirect object in the JSON format. The object contains two properties: redirect=true (which means that we want to perform a redirect on this action) and url (which contains the target URL). The [HttpPost] Edit method for the Edit view remains the same.

- The `Add` and `Remove` methods now take an additional `LibraryModel` argument. The argument stores the entire model obtained from the client (because Knockout MVC sends the entire model on each such requests). In the bodies of these methods, we update the static `Library` property with the client version of the model (let's recall that the static `Library` property symbolizes the main data source; for example, it can be a database in the real application).

Adding the view

Now let's discuss the most interesting part of our application—the view. We will start with the `Index` view:

```
@using PerpetuumSoft.Knockout
@model HomeLibrary3.Models.LibraryModel

@{
  ViewBag.Title = "HomeLibrary";
  var ko = Html.CreateKnockoutContext();
}

<div class="container">
  <h2 style="text-align: center">@ko.Html.Span(m => m.Name)</h2>
  <table class="table table-bordered table-striped table-condensed
    table-hover">
    <thead>
      <tr>
        <th>Title</th>
        <th>Author</th>
        <th>Year</th>
        <th>Actions</th>
      </tr>
    </thead>
    <tbody>
      @using (var book = ko.Foreach(m => m.Books))
      {
        <tr>
          <td>@book.Html.Span(m => m.Title)</td>
          <td>@book.Html.Span(m => m.Author)</td>
          <td>@book.Html.Span(m => m.Year)</td>
          <td>
```

```
          <a href="#" @ko.Bind.Click("EditRedirect", "Library",
            new { index = book.GetIndex() }) class="btn btn-
            primary btn-xs">Edit</a>
          <a href="#" @ko.Bind.Click("Remove", "Library", new {
            index = book.GetIndex() }) class="btn btn-primary
            btn-xs">Remove</a>
        </td>
      </tr>
    }
  </tbody>
</table>
<a href="#" @ko.Bind.Click("Add", "Library") class="btn btn-
  primary">Add new book</a>
</div>
```

```
@ko.Apply(Model)
```

Let's discuss the main differences this has from the native Knockout.js version from *Chapter 3, Integrating Knockout.js in ASP.NET MVC Applications.*

- Two typical Knockout MVC lines were added: `var ko = Html.CreateKnockoutContext();` and `@ko.Apply(Model)`.

- The JavaScript code has been completely removed! Now it will be automatically generated by the `ko.Apply` method.

- Bindings are declared via the `ko` object. For example, the binding to the `Name` property is declared as `@ko.Html.Span(m => m.Name)`.

- The `Foreach` are implemented using the `ko.Foreach` function. This function produces a nested context called `book` (working with contexts will be discussed in more detail in *Chapter 6, Advanced Features of Knockout MVC*; for now, we will limit ourselves to studying only the syntactic structure enumeration without understanding the internal logic). It means that we can bind to the `target` property of each book by using the `book` object instead of the `ko` object (for example, `@book.Html.Span(m => m.Title)`).

- The `Edit`, `Remove`, and `Add` hyperlinks use the `click` bindings via the `ko.Html.Click` method. Note that the `Edit` click event will occur with the `EditRedirect` method (it returns a special redirect object, which Knockout MVC takes and redirects the user to the Edit page). The `Remove` and `Add` click events use the usual `Remove` method (it will be performed by AJAX without a redirect or page reload).

The `Edit` view is almost identical to its previous version:

```
@model HomeLibrary3.Models.BookModel
@{ ViewBag.Title = "Edit book"; }
<div class="container">
  <h2 style="text-align: center">Edit book</h2>
  @using (Html.BeginForm("Edit", "Library", FormMethod.Post,
    new { @class = "form-horizontal", role = "form" }))
  {
    @Html.HiddenFor(m => m.Id)
    <div class="form-group">
      @Html.LabelFor(m => m.Title, new { @class = "col-sm-2
        control-label" })
      <div class="col-sm-10">
        @Html.TextBoxFor(m => m.Title, new { @class = "form-
          control" })
      </div>
    </div>
    <div class="form-group">
      @Html.LabelFor(m => m.Author, new { @class = "col-sm-2
        control-label" })
      <div class="col-sm-10">
        @Html.TextBoxFor(m => m.Author, new { @class = "form-
          control" })
      </div>
    </div>
    <div class="form-group">
      @Html.LabelFor(m => m.Year, new { @class = "col-sm-2
        control-label" })
      <div class="col-sm-10">
        @Html.TextBoxFor(m => m.Year, new { @class = "form-
          control" })
      </div>
    </div>
    <div class="form-group">
      <div class="col-sm-12">
        <input type="submit" class="btn btn-primary pull-right"
          value="Save" />
      </div>
    </div>
  }
</div>
```

Note that we added the hidden ID form field to store the ID of the edited book.

Running the application

Let's update `App_Start/RouteConfig.cs` with `controller = "Library"`, `action = "Index"` and run our `HomeLibrary3` application:

It looks exactly like `HomeLibrary2`, but the source code looks much more attractive. We got rid of the JavaScript code completely and moved all of our logic to the server side.

Under the hood

Let's look at the generated HTML code. The `ko.Apply` method gives us this very short JavaScript code:

```
<script type="text/javascript">
  var viewModelJs = {"Books":[{"Id":1,"Title":"Oliver
    Twist","Author":"Charles Dickens","Year":1837},
    {"Id":2,"Title":"Winnie-the-Pooh","Author":"A. A. Milne",
    "Year":1926},{"Id":3,"Title":"The Hobbit","Author":"J. R. R.
    Tolkien","Year":1937},{"Id":4,"Title":"The Bicentennial Man",
    "Author":"Isaac Asimov","Year":1976},{"Id":5,"Title":"The
    Green Mile","Author":"Stephen King","Year":1996}],
    "NextId":6,"Name":"My home library"};
  var viewModel = ko.mapping.fromJS(viewModelJs);
  ko.applyBindings(viewModel);
</script>
```

Here, we initialize the model in the JSON format, transform it to the Knockout.js model with the `knockout.mapping` plugin, and apply the bindings. Let's look to these bindings, which are as follows:

```html
<div class="container">
  <h2 style="text-align: center"><span data-bind="text : Name">
    </span></h2>
  <table class="table table-bordered table-striped table-condensed
    table-hover">
    <thead>
      <tr>
        <th>Title</th>
        <th>Author</th>
        <th>Year</th>
        <th>Actions</th>
      </tr>
    </thead>
    <tbody>
<!-- ko foreach: Books -->
        <tr>
          <td><span data-bind="text : $data.Title"></span></td>
          <td><span data-bind="text : $data.Author"></span></td>
          <td><span data-bind="text : $data.Year"></span></td>
          <td>
            <a href="#" data-bind="click : function()
              {executeOnServer(viewModel, '/Library/
              EditRedirect?index='+$index()+'');}" class="btn btn-
              primary btn-xs">Edit</a>
            <a href="#" data-bind="click : function()
              {executeOnServer(viewModel, '/Library/
              Remove?index='+$index()+'');}" class="btn btn-
              primary btn-xs">Remove</a>
          </td>
        </tr>
<!-- /ko -->
    </tbody>
  </table>
  <a href="#" data-bind="click : function()
    {executeOnServer(viewModel, '/Library/Add');}" class="btn btn-
    primary">Add new book</a>
</div>
```

The `name` binding is transformed in the simple `"text : Name"` line. `Foreach` was implemented by the `<!-- ko foreach: Books -->` construction. Do not hesitate to use bindings such as `"text : $data.Title"`. We will consider such construction in more detail in the next chapter. The `$data` term shows that the `text` property binds to the `Title` property of another book of the `foreach` loop. The `click` bindings in hyperlinks use the `executeOnServer` function from the Knockout MVC library. This function executes the target method on the server (as you may have guessed from the name), takes the response in the JSON format, and then applies the view using the new data, with the help of the `knockout.mapping` plugin. Also, this function can perform on another page (like in the `EditRedirect` case).

Summary

In this chapter, we got acquainted with the Knockout MVC library. This library can be very useful in certain cases for developing a simple ASP.NET MVC application, because it allows you to keep all business logic on the server and eliminates you from having to write client JavaScript code manually.

We started with a very simple "Hello World" application and discussed the basic Knockout MVC concepts. After that, we rewrote the `HomeLibrary` application from the previous chapter with a new approach. This helps us get away from the necessity to write JavaScript code because now we can develop our application (include model and logic) only on C#.

In the next two chapters, we will dive deeper into some useful features of native Knockout.js and its Knockout MVC wrapper. You can develop a simple Knockout.js and Knockout MVC application right now, but *Chapter 5*, *Advanced Features of Knockout.js*, and *Chapter 6*, *Advanced Features of Knockout MVC*, will help you better understand the structure of the libraries, and develop a really complicated web application with minimum effort.

5
Advanced Features of Knockout.js

Unfortunately, the basic features of Knockout.js are often not enough to write a really complex application. In this chapter, we will discuss some advanced features that may be useful in specific development scenarios. The features can be used in a pure Knockout.js application and in an application with server ASP.NET MVC logic. Also, understanding some of its features will help you understand how Knockout MVC works (see the next chapter for more details).

The list of topics that will be covered in this chapter is as follows:

- Loading and saving JSON data
- Mapping
- Binding context
- Custom bindings
- Extending observables
- Using `fn` to add custom functions
- Template binding

Loading and saving JSON data

In client-server applications, there are two very frequent tasks:

- Receiving data from the server
- Sending data to the server

These tasks need some format for data exchange. One of the most popular ways is using the JSON format (http://json.org/).

Generally, you can use any mechanism for data exchange operations, ranging from sending XMLHttpRequest and handling the response in pure JavaScript, to using third-party JS libraries and frameworks. It's very convenient to use the following jQuery's AJAX helper methods:

- getJSON: http://api.jquery.com/jQuery.getJSON/
- get: http://api.jquery.com/jQuery.get/
- post: http://api.jquery.com/jQuery.post/
- ajax: http://api.jquery.com/jQuery.ajax/

An example of data exchange is as follows:

```
// Receiving data from the server
$.getJSON("http://myserver.com", function(data) {
  // Here you can use received data
})

// Send data to the server
$.post("http://myserver.com", data, function(returnedData) {
  // Successful callback
})

// Using the ajax method
$.ajax({
  url: "http://myserver",
  context: document.body
}).done(function() {
  // Successful callback
});
```

Now, we need to solve two tasks: converting data to JSON and converting JSON to data.

Converting data to JSON

There are many ways to convert a JavaScript object to the JSON format. One of the most popular ways is using JSON.stringify (https://developer.mozilla.org/en-US/docs/JavaScript/Reference/Global_Objects/JSON/stringify).

It is a native function in most modern browsers. An example of this is as follows:

```
var model = { "LibraryName" : "My home library" };
JSON.stringify(model); // '{"LibraryName":"My home library"}'
```

However, this approach is not suitable for our case because the Knockout ViewModel contains observable properties (including computed observables, observable arrays, and so on). The reason why it is not possible to use JSON. stringify is that the observables are all the functions that can't be serialized correctly using JSON.stringify. That is why Knockout.js provides the following helper utility functions to serialize view model data into a JS object and JSON string:

- ko.toJS: It is a JavaScript object with a plain copy of your data and without Knockout artifacts
- ko.toJSON: It is a string JSON representation of the ko.toJS result

An example of using these is as follows:

```
var libraryViewModel = {
  LibraryName : ko.observable("My home library"),
  AmountOfBooks : ko.observable("5"),
};
libraryViewModel.HasBooks = ko.computed(function() {
  return this.AmountOfBooks() > 0
}, libraryViewModel)
var jsonObject = ko.toJS(libraryViewModel);
/*
jsonObject =
  {
    LibraryName: "My home library",
    AmountOfBooks: "5",
    HasBooks: true
  }
*/
var jsonString = ko.toJSON(libraryViewModel);
/*
jsonString = "{'LibraryName': 'My home library',
  'AmountOfBooks':'5','HasBooks':true}"
*/
```

Also, the `ko.toJSON` function can be very useful to debug your application (of course, there are other useful tools for debugging as well, for example, add-ons for modern web browsers). You can make a live representation of your ViewModel with the following HTML element:

```
<pre data-bind="text: ko.toJSON($root, null, 2)"></pre>
```

Converting JSON to data

If you already have some JSON strings and you want to convert them to a JSON object, the `JSON.parse` function (`https://developer.mozilla.org/en/docs/Web/JavaScript/Reference/Global_Objects/JSON/parse`) can help you. An example of this is as follows:

```
var jsonString = '{"LibraryName":"My home library",
  "AmountOfBooks":"5"}'; /* In the real application, we receive
  some data from the server*/
var jsonObject = JSON.parse(jsonString);
libraryViewModel.LibraryName(jsonObject.LibraryName);
libraryViewModel.AmountOfBooks(jsonObject.AmountOfBooks);
```

Introducing Knockout mapping

In this section, we will talk about the `knockout.mapping` plugin. This plugin allows you to map some plain JavaScript object to a Knockout.js ViewModel with observable properties. It can be very useful when you want to receive some data from the server in the JSON format and show it to the user via declarative bindings.

A manual mapping example

For better understanding of the mapping concept, let's consider an example with manual mapping of JSON data to a ViewModel object. We will take a very abridged version of the library model from the previous chapters. Suppose the model contains only two properties: `LibraryName` and `AmountOfBooks`.

1. Let's define a corresponding ViewModel:

```
var libraryViewModel = {
  LibraryName: ko.observable(),
  AmountOfBooks: ko.observable()
}
```

2. Next, we add a View:

```
The library <span data-bind="text: LibraryName"> contains
   <span data-bind="text: AmountOfBooks"> books.
```

3. Then, we should receive data from the server. Suppose we have a special `getModelFromServer` function for this purpose:

```
var libraryModel = getModelFromServer();
```

This function will get the model from the server via the AJAX request in the following form:

```
{
  LibraryName: "My home library",
  AmountOfBooks: "5"
}
```

4. After receiving data, we should update the ViewModel with the following code:

```
libraryViewModel.LibraryName(libraryModel.LibraryName);
libraryViewModel.AmountOfBooks(libraryModel.AmountOfBooks);
```

The application will work but this code is difficult to maintain due to the fact that it contains duplication. We will have to update the ViewModel definition and the manual data mapping logic per each update of the model structure.

An automatic mapping example

We can upgrade the manual example with the help of the `knockout.mapping` plugin.

> You can install the `knockout.mapping` plugin via NuGet using the following command:
>
> `Install-Package Knockout.Mapping`
>
> Alternatively, you can download the latest version of this plugin manually from GitHub (`https://github.com/SteveSanderson/knockout.mapping`). The plugin documentation is available on the official Knockout.js site (`http://knockoutjs.com/documentation/plugins-mapping.html`). Do not forget to add a link to the downloaded plugin in the main HTML layout template:
>
> ```
> <script src="@Url.Content("~/Scripts/knockout.mapping-
>     latest.js")" type="text/javascript"></script>
> ```

Now we are ready to use this plugin. You should replace the creation of the ViewModel with a simple line of code:

```
var libraryViewModel = ko.mapping.fromJS(libraryModel);
```

The `ko.mapping.fromJS` function automatically creates a ViewModel and defines an observable property for each property of the `libraryModel` object. Next, we should update the logic of receiving new data, as shown in the following code:

```
var libraryModel = getModelFromServer();
ko.mapping.fromJS(libraryModel, libraryViewModel);
```

As can be seen, the `ko.mapping.fromJS` function with two arguments can update an existing ViewModel with new data. Work is done and the application is ready.

Also, you can do the reverse operation with the `ko.mapping.toJS` function. It can be useful for sending processed data back to the server:

```
var libraryModel = ko.mapping.toJS(libraryViewModel);
sendModelToServer(libraryModel); // Perform some Ajax request
```

This operation is called **unmapping**.

Mapping in Knockout MVC

Now we can understand how Knockout MVC works. Let's remember the last example from *Chapter 4, Creating a Web Application with Knockout MVC*, in the *Under the hood* section:

```
<script type="text/javascript">
  var viewModelJs = {"Books":[{"Id":1,"Title":"Oliver Twist",
    "Author":"Charles Dickens","Year":1837},{"Id":2,"Title":
    "Winnie-the-Pooh","Author":"A. A. Milne","Year":1926},
    {"Id":3,"Title":"The Hobbit","Author":"J. R. R. Tolkien",
    "Year":1937},{"Id":4,"Title":"The Bicentennial Man",
    "Author":"Isaac Asimov","Year":1976},{"Id":5,"Title":"The
    Green Mile","Author":"Stephen King","Year":1996}],
    "NextId":6,"Name":"My home library"};
  var viewModel = ko.mapping.fromJS(viewModelJs);
  ko.applyBindings(viewModel);
</script>
```

In the preceding code, we defined a plain JSON object with the initial data and mapped it to a ViewModel object with the help of `ko.mapping.fromJS`. Data updating is also performed by the `knockout.mapping` plugin.

Mapping unique values

In this section, you will learn how to map unique values. Let's extend our model with the `Books` property:

```
var libraryModel = {
  Books: [
    { Id : 1, Title : "Oliver Twist" }
  ]
}
```

The steps are as follows:

1. Initially, we create a ViewModel using `ko.mapping.fromJS`:

   ```
   var libraryViewModel = ko.mapping.fromJS(libraryModel);
   ```

   Consider, for example, an admin decided to update the title of the book on the server with the original value, as follows:

   ```
   var libraryModel = {
     Books: [
       { Id : 1, Title : "Oliver Twist; or, The Parish Boy's
         Progress" }
     ]
   }
   ```

2. Next, we will receive new data from the server and update the ViewModel:

   ```
   ko.mapping.fromJS(libraryModel, libraryViewModel);
   ```

   However, there is a problem: the `{ Id : 1, Title : "Oliver Twist" }` book does not equal `{ Id : 1, Title : "Oliver Twist; or, The Parish Boy's Progress" }` as JSON objects. So, the update operation is performed by removing the old book item and adding a new book item. However, we only want to update the book item without any adding and removing.

   The `knockout.mapping` plugin is a great possibility to set some mapping options during the initialization of ViewModel.

3. We can use the `key` option to solve our problem. Options are defined by the following syntax:

   ```
   var mappingOptions = {
     'books': {
       key: function(model) {
   ```

```
                 return ko.utils.unwrapObservable(model.Id);
            }
         }
    }
    var libraryViewModel = ko.mapping.fromJS(libraryModel,
       mappingOptions);
```

The preceding code means that every update action will compare the old and new arrays by the `Id` property. So, in the considered example, the update operation will perform only the replacing of the old title of the book with the new value, without any changes of the array.

Partial mapping – create

In some scenarios, you would probably want to define your own mapping logic for some parts of a model. Let's consider an example: we want to create a special model for each book with additional properties. The `create` callback from mapping options helps us. Let's take the following model:

```
var libraryModel = {
  Books: [
    { Id : 1, Title : "Oliver Twist" }
  ]
}
```

Next, let's set mapping with special options using the following code:

```
var mappingOptions = {
  'books': {
    create: function(options) {
      return new bookModel(options.data);
    }
  }
}
var bookModel = function(model) {
    ko.mapping.fromJS(model, {}, this);
    this.TitleLength = ko.computed(function() {
        return this.Title().length;
    }, this);
}
var libraryViewModel = ko.mapping.fromJS(libraryModel,
  mappingOptions);
```

In the preceding code, we define the `create` callback for book creation. In the callback body, we create the `bookModel` object for each book. The `bookModel` function maps a book object in the usual way (the `ko.mapping.fromJS(model, {}, this);` line) and defines an additional computed observable property, `TitleLength`.

Partial mapping – update

In addition to the manually created mapped object, it will be very useful to be able to control the updating of the mapped data. We can do it with the `update` callback. Let's take the data as follows:

```
var libraryModel = {
  LibraryName: "My home library"
}
```

Now, define the `update` callback for the `LibraryName` property:

```
var mappingOptions = {
  "LibraryName": {
    update: function(options) {
      return """ + options.data + """;
    }
  }
}
var libraryViewModel = ko.mapping.fromJS(libraryModel,
  mappingOptions);
```

The preceding code adds the French quotation marks to `LibraryName`.

Partial mapping – ignore

In some scenarios, we don't need to map a whole model to a ViewModel. In this case, we can ignore the selected properties for the mapping operation:

```
var mappingOptions = {
  "ignore": ["LibraryName", "AmountOfBooks"]
}
var libraryViewModel = ko.mapping.fromJS(libraryModel,
  mappingOptions);
```

Alternatively, set the default `ignore` value for all mapping operations:

```
ko.mapping.defaultOptions().ignore = ["LibraryName",
  "AmountOfBooks"];
```

Multiple mappings

You can have several models that you want to use in the ViewModel. In this case, you can combine multiple models in one ViewModel by applying multiple `ko.mapping.fromJS` calls:

```
var libraryViewModel = ko.mapping.fromJS(library1Model,
  library1MappingOptions);
ko.mapping.fromJS(library2Model, library2MappingOptions,
  libraryViewModel);
```

Advanced mapping

The `knockout.mapping` plugin also supports some advanced possibilities to fine-tune mapping operations.

 You can find the actual full list of plugin features in the documentation section on the official site at `http://knockoutjs.com/documentation/plugins-mapping.html`.

Binding context

`Binding contexts` are a hierarchical structure of special objects that help you make logical scopes for the control flow bindings. Each such binding (such as `foreach`, `if`, `with`, and so on) generates its own binding context in the hierarchy. You can think of contexts as a scoped wrapper of a ViewModel. For example, the root binding context refers to your main ViewModel. You can work with contexts with the help of special properties that are listed as follows. The best way to understand the binding context concept is to look at some examples. Let's do it.

- `$parent`: This refers to the ViewModel of the parent binding context. For example, say you have the `foreach` binding to the book collection, but want to use the name of the library inside `foreach`. The parent context helps you as follows:

```
<div data-bind="foreach: Books">
  The book "<span data-bind="text: Name"></span>" from the
    "<span data-bind="text: $parent.LibraryName"></span>"
    library.
</div>
```

- $parents: This refers to an array with a full binding context ViewM~
  stack. So, you can write $parents[0] (it means $parent), $parents[1]
  (the parent of the parent), …, $parents[i] (the parent of $parents[i-1]),
  and so on.

- $root: This refers to the ViewModel of the root binding context (main
  ViewModel). It also corresponds to the last element of the $parents array.

- $index: This works only within the foreach binding and refers to the
  index of the current item in the enumerated collection. An example of
  this is as follows:

```
<ul data-bind="foreach: ['Oliver Twist', ''Winnie-the-
  Pooh', 'The hobbit']">
  <li>Book index: <span data-bind="text:
    $index"></span></li>
</ul>
```

- $parentContext: This refers to the parent binding context (unlike
  $parent, which refers to the ViewModel of the parent binding context).
  For example, you can write $parentContext.$index for access to $index
  of $parentContext ($index is a property of the binding context, not the
  corresponding ViewModel).

- $data: This refers to the ViewModel of the current binding context. An
  example of this is as follows:

```
<ul data-bind="foreach: ['Oliver Twist', ''Winnie-the-
  Pooh', 'The hobbit']">
  <li>Book name: <span data-bind="text: $data"></span></li>
</ul>
```

- $context: This refers to the current binding context (unlike $data,
  which refers to the ViewModel of the current binding context).

- $element: This refers to the current DOM element. An example of this
  is as follows:

```
<div id="LibraryNameDiv" data-bind="text:
  $element.id"></div>
```

Custom bindings

In *Chapter 2, Creating a Simple Knockout.js Application*, we examined a variety of
standard Knockout.js bindings such as text, visible, click, submit, and so on.
However, in a big application, this list may not be enough. Fortunately, you can
define your own custom bindings.

Registering a new binding

Knockout.js provides us with the `ko.bindingHandlers` property to register
new bindings. You can define a new subproperty of it as a JavaScript object with
two callback properties: `init` and `update`. Let's take a look at the short binding
registration template:

```
ko.bindingHandlers.newBindingName = {
    init: function(element, valueAccéssor, allBindings) {
        // Called on first binding applying to an element
        // Set up any initial state
    },
    update: function(element, valueAccessor, allBindings) {
        // Called on first binding applying to an element and on
            any changing in dependences
        // Update the DOM element
    }
};
```

You can apply such bindings to any DOM elements (you must define at least one of
the `init` and `update` callbacks):

```
<div data-bind="newBindingName: specificValue"></div>
```

Binding callbacks' parameters

The `init` and `update` callbacks support the following parameters:

- `element`: This is a target DOM element that is used for binding.

- `valueAccessor`: This is an accessor to the target property (for example,
  a call without parameters gives the property value for the current model).

- `allBindings`: This is an accessor to all model values bound to a target
  DOM element (for example, the expressions `allBindings.has("name")`
  and `allBindings.get("name")` allow to operate with the value of the
  `name` binding).

Also, callbacks support advanced parameters (for example, the `bindingContext`
parameter to work with contexts), but they are rarely used in real applications.
The full description of parameters is available in the official documentation
(`http://knockoutjs.com/documentation/custom-bindings.html`).

A custom binding example 1 – slideVisible

Let's consider an example from the official documentation. We will create the custom `slideVisible` binding as an animated version of the usual `visible` binding with the help of the `slideUp` and `slideDown` jQuery functions, as shown in the following code:

```
ko.bindingHandlers.slideVisible = { // 1
  init: function(element, valueAccessor) { // 2
    var value = valueAccessor(); // 3
    var valueUnwrapped = ko.unwrap(value); // 4
    $(element).toggle(valueUnwrapped); // 5
  },
  update: function(element, valueAccessor, allBindings) { // 6
    var value = valueAccessor(); // 7
    var valueUnwrapped = ko.unwrap(value); // 8
    var duration = allBindings.get('slideDuration') || 400; // 9
    if (valueUnwrapped == true) // 10
      $(element).slideDown(duration); // 11
    else
      $(element).slideUp(duration); //12
  }
};
```

Let's examine this code in detail (item numbers correspond to numbers in comments):

1. Start of new `slideVisible` bindings definition.

2. Start of the `init` callback definition. It takes only two parameters (`element` and `valueAccessor`) because we don't need other parameters in this example.

3. Receive the observable property value.

4. Receive the plain value from the observable value with the help of the `ko.unwrap` function.

5. Set the initial visibility of the target DOM element with the help of the `toggle` jQuery function. It hides or shows the element depending on the plain property value.

6. Start of the `update` callback definition. It takes three parameters (`element`, `valueAccessor`, and `allBindings`).

7. The same as the point 3.

8. The same as the point 4.

9. Receive the value of the `slideDuration` parameter via `allBindings`. In an undefined case, `400` will be used.

10. Check the plain property value.

11. If the `slideVisibile` value is `true`, show the element with the help of the `slideDown` jQuery function.

12. If the `slideVisibile` value is `false`, hide the element with help of the `slideUp` jQuery function.

Next, let's use the defined binding in a view:

```
<div data-bind="slideVisible: giftWrap, slideDuration:600"> <!-- 1 -->
  You have selected the option
</div>
<label>
  <input type="checkbox" data-bind="checked: giftWrap" /> <!-- 2 -->
  Gift wrap
</label>

<script type="text/javascript">
  var viewModel = { <!-- 3 -->
    giftWrap: ko.observable(true) <!-- 4 -->
  };
  ko.applyBindings(viewModel); <!-- 5 -->
</script>
```

The view in detail is explained as follows:

1. Applying the `slideVisible` binding to the `div` element. The value of the binding is the `giftWrap` property of the ViewModel. Also, the binding contains the additional `slideDuration` parameter with a value of `600`.

2. Applying the `checked` binding to a checkbox. The value of the binding is also the `giftWrap` property of the ViewModel. Therefore, both bindings link to the same property. The initial value is `true` (we will see the target element).

3. Start of the ViewModel definition.

4. Definition of the main and the only ViewModel boolean property called `giftWrap`.

5. Applying bindings to the ViewModel.

This example demonstrates the basics of using custom bindings very well. You can use the created `slideVisible` binding many times for different elements.

A custom binding example 2 – hasFocus

The second example helps to understand how you can use the custom bindings for the creation of dynamic behavior based on events. Let's define a new custom binding called `hasFocus`, as shown in the following code:

```
ko.bindingHandlers.hasFocus = { // 1
  init: function(element, valueAccessor) { //2
    $(element).focus(function() { // 3
      var value = valueAccessor(); // 4
      value(true); // 5
    });
    $(element).blur(function() { // 6
      var value = valueAccessor(); // 7
      value(false); // 8
    });
  },
  update: function(element, valueAccessor) { // 9
    var value = valueAccessor(); // 10
    var valueUnwrapped = ko.unwrap(value); // 11
    if (valueUnwrapped) // 12
      element.focus(); // 13
    else
      element.blur(); // 14
  }
};
```

The explanation of the code in detail is as follows:

1. Start of the new `hasFocus` binding definition.
2. Start of the `init` callback definition with two parameters (`element` and `valueAccessor`).
3. Register an event handler for the `focus` jQuery event.
4. Receive the observable property value.
5. Set the `true` value via an accessor (element gets focus).
6. Register an event handler for the `blur` jQuery event.
7. Receive the observable property value.
8. Set the `false` value via an accessor (element loses focus).
9. Start of the `update` callback definition with two parameters (`element` and `valueAccessor`).
10. Receive the observable property value.

11. Receive the plain value from the observable value with the help of the `ko.unwrap` function.

12. Check the plain property value.

13. If the `hasFocus` value is `true`, set the focus for the element.

14. If the `hasFocus` value is `false`, reset the focus from the element.

The View will be as follows:

```
<p>
  Name:
  <input data-bind="hasFocus: editingName" /> <!-- 1 -->
</p>
<div data-bind="visible: editingName"> <!-- 2 -->
  You're editing the name
</div>
<button data-bind="enable: !editingName(), click:function() {
  editingName(true) }"> <!-- 3 -->
  Edit name
</button>
<script type="text/javascript">
  var viewModel = { <!-- 4 -->
    editingName: ko.observable() <!-- 5 -->
  };
    ko.applyBindings(viewModel); <!-- 6 -->
</script>
```

The view in detail is explained as follows:

1. Applying the `hasFocus` binding to the `input` element. The value of the binding is the `editingName` property of the model. It means that `editingName` is equal to `true` only if the input element has the focus.

2. Applying the `visible` binding to the `text` element. The value of the binding is also `editingName`. It means that the user will see the `text` element only if the `input` element has focus.

3. Applying two bindings to the `button` element. The first binding (`enable: !editingName()`) means that the button will be enabled only if a user finishes editing (the `input` element does not have focus). The second binding (`click: function() { editingName(true) }`) means that the click of the button sets the focus on the `input` element.

4. Start of the ViewModel definition.

5. Definition of the main and the only ViewModel boolean property called `editingName`.

6. Applying bindings with the ViewModel.

Extending observables

Observables are a very useful and powerful part of Knockout.js. They allow you to create flexible and reliable applications. However, sometimes, you need to *extend* the opportunities of your observable properties. The **extenders** help you! As usual, let's proceed with some examples from the official documentation in detail.

Creating an extender

In this section, we will write a simple extender, as follows:

```
ko.extenders.logChange = function(target, option) { // 1
  target.subscribe(function(newValue) { // 2
    console.log(option + ": " + newValue); // 3
  });
  return target; // 4
};
```

Let's discuss it in detail:

1. We use the `ko.extenders` object to create a new extender by adding a new property. In the preceding example, the property name is `logChange`. This extender will log any changes of the target binding value. In fact, an extender is just a function with two parameters. The first parameter (`target`) is the observable itself, the second parameter (`option`) is any option to define an extender.

2. We use the `subscribe` function of the target binding to subscribe to its changes. The single parameter of the `subscribe` function is a callback that receives a new binding value.

3. This is our main logic: we log information about the changing of values to the console. In this example, `option` is just a user-defined name for an extender instance.

4. Finally, we return the binding. Each extender should return an observable. Usually, it returns the original `target` observable (as in our case), but it can also be a computed observable based on `target`.

Now we are ready for the View:

```
this.firstName = ko.observable("Bob").extend({logChange: "first
  name"});
```

This is a very simple single line of JavaScript code. We create a new observable (with the initial value "Bob") and *extend* it using the `logChange` extender with option as "first name". Now, any changes of the `firstName` observable produces a logging message to the console.

An extending observables example 1 – numeric

Let's take a real-world problem. In some applications, a user needs to work with fractional numbers, but we don't really need high precision in all cases. In most cases, we need a fixed number of digits after the decimal point. Let's write an extender for this problem:

```
ko.extenders.numeric = function(target, precision) { // 1
  var result = ko.pureComputed({ // 2
    read: target, // 3
    write: function(newValue) { // 4
      var current = target(), // 5
        roundingMultiplier = Math.pow(10, precision), // 6
        newValueAsNum = isNaN(newValue) ? 0 : parseFloat
          (+newValue), // 7
        valueToWrite = Math.round(newValueAsNum *
          roundingMultiplier) / roundingMultiplier; // 8
      if (valueToWrite !== current) { // 9
        target(valueToWrite); // 10
      } else {
        if (newValue !== current) { // 11
          target.notifySubscribers(valueToWrite); // 12
        }
      }
    }
  }).extend({ notify: 'always' }); // 13
  result(target()); // 14
  return result; // 15
};

// ViewModel
function AppViewModel(one, two) { // 16
  this.myNumberOne = ko.observable(one).extend({ numeric: 0 }); //
    17
```

```
    this.myNumberTwo = ko.observable(two).extend({ numeric: 2 }); //
       18
}

ko.applyBindings(new AppViewModel(221.2234, 123.4525)); // 19

<!-- View --> <!-- 20 -->
<p>
   <input data-bind="value: myNumberOne" /> <!-- 21 -->
   (round to whole number)
</p>
<p>
   <input data-bind="value: myNumberTwo" /> <!-- 22 -->
   (round to two decimals)
</p>
```

Let's discuss this snippet in detail:

1. We create a new extender called `numeric`. The corresponding function will take two parameters: `target` (the binding) and `precision` (our option).
2. We use the `ko.pureComputed` function to create a new writeable computed observable. It will be an intercept write operation of the `target` observable.
3. Set a read function for the created computed observable. It will just return the original binding.
4. Set a write function. The function will include some logic to transform the original new binding value to its rounded version.
5. First, we call `target()` to get the current value of the `target` binding.
6. Next, we calculate `10^precision` and store the result in `roundingMultiplier`.
7. If the new value is `NaN`, we assume that the value is zero. Otherwise, we parse a new value as a float.
8. Now we are ready to round the value. In order to obtain the desired precision, we multiply the value by `roundingMultiplier`, round it, and then divide it by `roundingMultiplier`. It is the usual way to get the number rounded with a fixed number of digits after the decimal point.
9. Next, we compare the current value and the rounded new value.
10. If they are not equal, we update the `target` binding by the rounded new value.

11. If they are equal, we should compare the current value and the original new value.

12. If they are not equal, we should notify the subscribers about the new value without an explicit `target` update.

13. Finally, we extend the new pure computed observable by the `notify` extender with the `always` value; it forces the deletion of the rejected values.

14. Initialization of the newly created pure compound observable.

15. As a result, the `numeric` extender will return the newly created observable.

16. Now we define a ViewModel for our application. It will contain two float numbers.

17. The first number is a float observable that is extended by the `numeric` extender with zero precision. It means that the number will actually be an integer.

18. The second number is also a float observable, but we will use the `numeric` extender with precision `2` for it. It means that the number will keep only two digits after the decimal point.

19. We apply bindings with the newly defined ViewModel. The ViewModel constructor takes two parameters, that is, its initial values for the ViewModel numbers.

20. Now we start with the View.

21. One input element for the first number.

22. Another input element for the second number.

If you run the application, you will see two textboxes with limited numbers of digits after the decimal point. The new `numeric` extender is reusable; we can apply it for everything we want.

An extending observables example 2 – required

Let's look at another example for a better understanding of extenders. The data validation is a common requirement in many applications. One such requirement is the required fields, that is, fields that are required to have a non-empty value. So, let's write the application with a new extender for this purpose:

```
ko.extenders.required = function(target, overrideMessage) { // 1
    target.hasError = ko.observable(); // 2
```

```
  target.validationMessage = ko.observable(); // 3

  function validate(newValue) { // 4
     target.hasError(newValue ? false : true); // 5
     target.validationMessage(newValue
       ? ""
       : overrideMessage || "This field is required"); // 6
  }

  validate(target()); // 7

  target.subscribe(validate); // 8

  return target; // 9
};


// ViewModel
function AppViewModel(first, last) { // 10
  this.firstName = ko.observable(first).
    extend({ required: "Please enter a first name" }); // 11
  this.lastName = ko.observable(last).
    extend({ required: "" }); // 12
}

ko.applyBindings(new AppViewModel("Bob","Smith")); // 13

<!-- View --> <!-- 14 -->
<p data-bind="css: { error: firstName.hasError }"> <!-- 15 -->
  <input data-bind=
    'value: firstName, valueUpdate: "afterkeydown"' /> <!-- 16 -->
  <span data-bind='visible: firstName.hasError, text:
    firstName.validationMessage'></span> <-- 17 -->
</p>
<p data-bind="css: { error: lastName.hasError }"> <!-- 18 -->
  <input data-bind=
    'value: lastName, valueUpdate: "afterkeydown"' /> <!-- 19 -->
  <span data-bind='visible: lastName.hasError, text:
    lastName.validationMessage'> </span> <!-- 20 -->
</p>
```

Let's discuss this snippet in detail:

1. We create a new extender called `required`. In this case, the option will be called `overrideMessage`. It will be used as a specific text value with an error message about an empty field.

2. We add a new subobservable property for the target observable. The first subobservable is an error flag.

3. The second subobservable is a result validation message.

4. Now, we need a validation function. It takes `newValue` as a single parameter.

5. If `newValue` is empty (in JavaScript, an empty string is `false`), set `hasError` to `true`; otherwise, set it to `false`.

6. If `newValue` is empty, we should also set `validationMessage` (if it's not empty) as `overrideMessage` or the default `This field is required` message; otherwise, we should set it to an empty string.

7. This is the initial validation.

8. We add the validation function as a subscriber to the `target` binding.

9. Finally, the extender returns the `target` binding (with some modifications).

10. Now is the time for the ViewModel. It will contain two strings: the first name and the last name of a person.

11. An observable property for the first name is extended by the `required` observable with the `Please enter a first name` message.

12. An observable property for the second name is extended by the required observable without a specific error message.

13. Apply binding to the ViewModel. The initial name of the person is Bob Smith.

14. Now, we start with the View.

15. It is the first paragraph for the first name. If the `firstName` binding contains an error, the `error` style will be applied to the paragraph.

16. This is an input element for the first name. Its text binds to the `firstName` property with the `afterkeydown` update.

17. The error message for the first name. It would be visible if, and only if, the textbox is empty.

18. The same as point 15 for the second name.

19. The same as point 16 for the second name.

20. The same as point 17 for the second name.

As a result, we get an application with two textboxes for the first
name of a person. If the first textbox is empty, the "Please ente~
will be shown. If the second textbox is empty, the default "Th.
message will be shown.

You can write your own extenders and apply them multiple times i.
application. It is useful to keep in mind that several extenders can be a~
by a single line like this:

```
this.firstName = ko.observable(first).extend({ required: "Pleas
    enter a first name", logChange: "first name" });
```

You can also use an existing Knockout.js plugin for validation, available at
`https://github.com/ericmbarnard/Knockout-Validation`.

Custom functions

Knockout.js allows you to write your own custom functions to extend the capabilities
of a standard Knockout.js object. The following objects from the Knockout.js
hierarchy can be extended:

- `ko.subscribable` (root object)
- `ko.computed` (inherited from `ko.subscribable`)
- `ko.observable` (inherited from `ko.subscribable`)
- `ko.observableArray` (inherited from `ko.observable`)

If you write a custom function for an object, the inheritors of the object will also have
the written function. For example, you can use a custom function of `ko.observable`
with `ko.observableArray`.

An example with array filtering

Let's learn how to write a custom function with the following example. We will write
the `filterByProperty` function for `ko.observableArray`. This function will filter
the original array and keep only those items for which the specified property is equal
to the specified value. The function body is as follows:

```
ko.observableArray.fn.filterByProperty = function(propName,
    matchValue) {
    return ko.computed(function() {
        var allItems = this(), matchingItems = [];
        for (var i = 0; i < allItems.length; i++) {
```

```
      var current = allItems[i];
      if (ko.unwrap(current[propName]) === matchValue)
        matchingItems.push(current);
    }
    return matchingItems;
  }, this);
}
```

Now, let's use it. For example, we want to divide books in our library into two groups: read and unread.

The **ViewModel** will be as follows:

```
function Book(title, read) {
  this.title = ko.observable(title);
  this.read = ko.observable(read);
}
function LibraryViewModel() {
  this.books = ko.observableArray([
    new Book('Oliver Twist', true),
    new Book('Winnie-the-Pooh', false),
    new Book('The Hobbit', true),
    new Book('The Bicentennial Man', false),
    new Book('The Green Mile', true)
  ]);
  this.readBooks = this.books.filterByProperty("read", true);
  this.unreadBooks = this.books.filterByProperty("read", false);
}
ko.applyBindings(new LibraryViewModel());
```

The **View** will be as follows:

```
<h3>All books (<span data-bind="text: books().length">
  </span>)</h3>
<ul data-bind="foreach: books">
  <li>
    <label>
      <input type="checkbox" data-bind="checked: read" />
      <span data-bind="text: title"> </span>
    </label>
  </li>
</ul>
```

```
<h3>Read books (<span data-bind="text: readBooks().length">
  </span>)</h3>
<ul data-bind="foreach: readBooks">
  <li data-bind="text: title"></li>
</ul>

<h3>Unread books (<span data-bind="text: unreadBooks().length">
  </span>)</h3>
<ul data-bind="foreach: unreadBooks">
  <li data-bind="text: title"></li>
</ul>
```

The result is as shown in the following screenshot:

Let's discuss the preceding example in detail:

- `filterByProperty`: We defined the custom function for `ko.observableArray` with the `ko.observableArray.fn` extensibility points. The `fn` helps to write a custom function for any Knockout.js object. The `filterByProperty` function takes two arguments: the name of the target property (`propName`) and the target property value for filtering (`matchValue`). The function body is very simple. We just select matched items from the original array and build a new array with the selected items.

- `Book`: In this example, the book model contains only two properties: the string book `title` and the boolean flag `read` (`true` for a read book and `false` for an unread book).

- `LibraryViewModel`: The first property of the ViewModel is the observable array for books. The ViewModel also has two additional observable arrays for read and unread books. We build these arrays with help of the `filterByProperty` function of the `books` array. The first function argument is `read` because we filter the original array by this property. The second argument is `true` for read books and `false` for unread books.

- In the View, we define three lists: for all books, for read books, and for unread books. Each list uses the corresponding property of the ViewModel (`books`, `readBooks`, and `unreadBooks`). The first list item also has the checkbox to manipulate the `read` flag.

Therefore, the custom function is a powerful approach, which allows you to write reusable code by extending the standard Knockout.js object with some custom logic.

Also, there are some useful utility functions in Knockout.js such as `arrayFilter` (see `http://www.knockmeout.net/2011/04/utility-functions-in-knockoutjs.html`).

Different templating approaches

Knockout.js provides you with great opportunities to write reusable code. Another important task is writing reusable markup. This task can be solved with the help of named templates. It is a very convenient way to create a flexible view. We already discussed one template approach with the control flow bindings (`foreach`, `if`, and `with`). In this section, we will discuss another approach: the string-based templates. They help you connect Knockout.js with third-party templates' engines. The following parameters can be useful in such a case:

- `name`: This is the name of the defined template
- `data`: This is a model for the template
- `if`: This is a condition under which the template will be rendered
- `foreach`: This is a model for the template in the "foreach" mode
- `as`: This is an alias for the template in the "foreach" mode

As usual, we will learn about the template mechanism with examples.

A simple named template

In the first example, we will just cover how to create a simple named template.
Let's create a template for a book and call it `book-template`.

The template is as follows:

```html
<script type="text/html" id="book-template">
  <h3 data-bind="text: title"></h3>
  <p>Author: <span data-bind="text: author"></span></p>
  <p>Year: <span data-bind="text: year"></span></p>
</script>
```

It is a simple HTML markup in the `script` element with `id="book-template"`.
This markup tells us how book information should be rendered.

Next, we will define a ViewModel with information about two books.

The ViewModel will be as follows:

```javascript
<script type="text/javascript">
  function LibraryViewModel() {
    this.book1 = { title: 'Oliver Twist', author: 'Charles
      Dickens', year: 1837 };
    this.book2 = { title: 'Winnie-the-Pooh', author: 'A. A.
      Milne', year: 1926 };
    this.book3 = { title: 'The Hobbit', author: 'J. R. R.
      Tolkien', year: 1937 };
  }
  ko.applyBindings(new LibraryViewModel());
</script>
```

In this example, we defined books as separate ViewModel properties. We specifically
did not use an observable array because our current task is just learning how named
templates work. Finally, we will define our View.

The View will be as follows:

```html
<div data-bind="template: { name: 'book-template', data: book1
  }"></div>
<div data-bind="template: { name: 'book-template', data: book2
  }"></div>
<div data-bind="template: { name: 'book-template', data: book2
  }"></div>
```

The View includes the three div elements, one per book. We don't need to write our own markup for each book, we can just use the defined template. The name property refers to the template by name, and the data property refers to the target ViewModel property.

Template in the foreach mode

If we have an array, templates can help us render each element of the array with the foreach template property. Let's rewrite the previous example in such a way. The template will remain unchanged.

The template is as follows:

```html
<script type="text/html" id="book-template">
  <h3 data-bind="text: title"></h3>
  <p>Author: <span data-bind="text: author"></span></p>
  <p>Year: <span data-bind="text: year"></span></p>
</script>
```

The ViewModel will be rewritten with the JavaScript array.

The ViewModel will be as follows:

```html
<script type="text/javascript">
  function LibraryViewModel() {
    this.books = [
      { title: 'Oliver Twist', author: 'Charles Dickens', year:
        1837 },
      { title: 'Winnie-the-Pooh', author: 'A. A. Milne', year:
        1926 },
      { title: 'The Hobbit', author: 'J. R. R. Tolkien', year:
        1937 }
    ]
  }
  ko.applyBindings(new LibraryViewModel());
</script>
```

Finally, we can render the whole array using a single div element with the foreach binding.

The View will be as follows:

```html
<div data-bind="template: { name: 'book-template', foreach: books
  }"></div>
```

It is very similar to the situation when we rendered arrays with the foreach binding without templates. However, now we learn how to separate the view of a book from the main View.

The foreach template with alias

Sometimes, you need to refer to the element in the foreach loop. It is a very frequent task in a hierarchical layout with nested foreach loops. Earlier, we solved this problem with a binding context. In the template method, you can use aliases for the foreach element with the help of the as binding. For example, we want to set the character list for each book.

The ViewModel will be as follows:

```
<script type="text/javascript">
  function LibraryViewModel() {
    this.books = [
      { title: 'Oliver Twist', characters: [ 'Fagin', 'Nancy' ] },
      { title: 'Winnie-the-Pooh', characters: [ 'Owl', 'Rabbit' ]
        },
      { title: 'The Hobbit', characters: [ 'Bilbo', 'Gandalf' ] }
    ]
  }
  ko.applyBindings(new LibraryViewModel());
</script>
```

Let's define two templates: one for a book and one for a character. The second template will be nested to the first one.

The templates are as follows:

```
<script type="text/html" id="book-template">
  <li>
    <strong data-bind="text: title"></strong>
    <ul data-bind="template: { name: 'character-template',
      foreach: characters, as: 'character' }"></ul>
  </li>
</script>

<script type="text/html" id="character-template">
  <li>
    <span data-bind="text: character"></span> is a character in
      the "<span data-bind="text: book.title"></span>" book
  </li>
</script>
```

The View will be as follows:

```
<ul data-bind="template: { name: 'book-template', foreach: books,
   as: 'book' }"></ul>
```

The View contains a single `ul` element for the rendering of the books array. This element uses `book-template` to render a view for the books array. We used the `as` binding to create an element alias (`book`). Next, there is the nested `ul` element in `book-template`. This element uses `character-template` to render the view for the characters array for each book. The `as` binding sets alias for an element in the character array. Finally, we used the defined aliases in the `character-template`: `data-bind="text: character"` to display the character name, and `data-bind="text: book.title"` to display the book title.

Choosing a template dynamically

In some situations, we need several templates for a model, where each template will be used for a particular case. For example, a book can have a status as read or unread. Also, we want to use different templates for books with different statuses. Let's define two templates for each case.

The templates are as follows:

```
<script type="text/html" id="book-template-read">
  <h3 data-bind="text: title"></h3>
  <p>Status: read</p>
</script>

<script type="text/html" id="book-template-unread">
  <h3 data-bind="text: title"></h3>
  <p>Status: unread</p>
</script>
```

Next, we should define the ViewModel. We will extend our books array with an additional function. This function will choose the target template for the book.

The View will be as follows:

```
<script type="text/javascript">
  function LibraryViewModel() {
    this.books = [
      { title: 'Oliver Twist', read: true },
      { title: 'Winnie-the-Pooh', read: false },
```

```
        { title: 'The Hobbit', read: true }
    ]
    this.readStatus = function(book) {
      return book.read ? "book-template-read" : "boo
        unread";
    }
  }
  ko.applyBindings(new LibraryViewModel());
</script>
```

Finally, we will define the View. We will use the `readStatus` function (this functio...
returns the target template name) instead of a constant template name.

The View will be as follows:

```
<div data-bind="template: { name: readStatus, foreach: books
  }"></div>
```

As a result, each book will be rendered with its own template according to the
book status.

Summary

In this chapter, we covered a huge number of useful Knockout.js possibilities to
create powerful applications.

We also discussed how to exchange the data between the client and server with
the JSON format. The mapping plugin provides us with an easy way to use JSON
data in the Knockout.js ViewModel with the observables properties.

Now, we know how to create complex hierarchical markup with the help of
binding contexts. We can define our own custom bindings in addition to the
standard Knockout.js bindings. Moreover, we can extend the basic functionality with
the help of the binding extenders and custom functions for the Knockout.js objects.

Finally, we saw how to define flexible and reusable HTML markup with templates.

All of these approaches allow us to use the full power of the Knockout.js framework
and create really great applications.

6

Advanced Features of Knockout MVC

In this chapter, you'll learn how to use advanced Knockout MVC features.
You can develop a simple application with only basic Knockout MVC capabilities.
However, any real application needs special concepts, such as **regions**, **complex bindings**, **combined contexts**, and so on. You may need to transfer some parameters to the server, write your own user scripts, or perform lazy loading of your data in the case of big data.

The topics that will be covered in this chapter are as follows:

- Regions
- Complex bindings
- Sending parameters to the server
- Inner computed properties
- Lazy loading
- Multiple view models
- User scripts

Regions

Knockout MVC regions provide you with the **Razor API** to use Knockout.js control flow binding, such as `if`, `foreach`, and `with`. In this section, you will learn how to create these elements without JavaScript code.

The foreach region

The `foreach` region allows you to iterate over some collections with nice Razor syntax. Let's implement our usual library example in Knockout MVC:

The **Model** will be as follows:

```
public class BookModel
{
  public string Title { get; set; }
  public string Author { get; set; }
  public int Year { get; set; }
}
public class LibraryModel
{
  public List<BookModel> Books { get; set; }
}
```

The **Controller** will be as follows:

```
public class LibraryController : KnockoutController
{
  public ActionResult Index()
  {
    var model = new LibraryModel
    {
      Books = new List<BookModel>
      {
          new BookModel { Title = "Oliver Twist", Author =
            "Charles Dickens", Year = 1837 },
          new BookModel { Title = "Winnie-the-Pooh", Author = "A.
            A. Milne", Year = 1926 },
          new BookModel { Title = "The Hobbit", Author = "J. R. R.
            Tolkien", Year = 1937 },
      }
    };
    return View(model);
  }
}
```

The **View** (Razor) will be as follows:

```
@using PerpetuumSoft.Knockout
@model KnockoutMvcDemo.Models.LibraryModel
@{
```

```
    var ko = Html.CreateKnockoutContext();
}
<table>
  <tr>
    <th>Title</th>
    <th>Author</th>
    <th>Year</th>
  </tr>
  @using (var books = ko.Foreach(m => m.Books))
  {
    <tr>
      <td @books.Bind.Text(book => book.Title)></td>
      <td @books.Bind.Text(book => book.Author)></td>
      <td @books.Bind.Text(book => book.Year)></td>
    </tr>
  }
</table>
@ko.Apply(Model)
```

The **View** (Generated) will be as follows:

```
<table>
  <tr>
    <th>Title</th>
    <th>Author</th>
    <th>Year</th>
  </tr>
<!-- ko foreach: Books -->
    <tr>
      <td data-bind="text : $data.Title"></td>
      <td data-bind="text : $data.Author"></td>
      <td data-bind="text : $data.Year"></td>
    </tr>
<!-- /ko -->
</table>
<script type="text/javascript">
var viewModelJs = {"Books":[{"Title":"Oliver Twist","Author":
  "Charles Dickens","Year":1837},{"Title":"Winnie-the-Pooh",
  "Author":"A. A. Milne","Year":1926},{"Title":"The Hobbit",
  "Author":"J. R. R. Tolkien","Year":1937}]};
var viewModel = ko.mapping.fromJS(viewModelJs);
ko.applyBindings(viewModel);
</script>
```

We use the `@using (var books = ko.Foreach(m => m.Books))` statement to iterate over the book list. As you can see, this instruction transforms into the usual Knockout.js `foreach` binding:

```
<!-- ko foreach: Books -->
    <tr>
      <td data-bind="text : $data.Title"></td>
      <td data-bind="text : $data.Author"></td>
      <td data-bind="text : $data.Year"></td>
    </tr>
<!-- /ko -->
```

The with region

The `with` region is a wrapper for the `with` Knockout.js binding. Let's update the previous example by creating a separate variable for the book inside the `foreach` loop.

The **Model** will be as follows:

```
public class BookModel
{
  public string Title { get; set; }
  public string Author { get; set; }
  public int Year { get; set; }
}
public class LibraryModel
{
  public List<BookModel> Books { get; set; }
}
```

The **Controller** will be as follows:

```
public class LibraryController : KnockoutController
{
  public ActionResult Index()
  {
    var model = new LibraryModel
    {
      Books = new List<BookModel>
      {
          new BookModel { Title = "Oliver Twist", Author =
            "Charles Dickens", Year = 1837 },
```

```
        new BookModel { Title = "Winnie-the-Pooh", Author = "A.
          A. Milne", Year = 1926 },
        new BookModel { Title = "The Hobbit", Author = "J. R. R.
          Tolkien", Year = 1937 },
      }
    };
    return View(model);
  }
}
```

The **View** (Razor) will be as follows:

```
@using PerpetuumSoft.Knockout
@model KnockoutMvcDemo.Models.LibraryModel
@{
  var ko = Html.CreateKnockoutContext();
}
<table>
  <tr>
    <th>Title</th>
    <th>Author</th>
    <th>Year</th>
  </tr>
  @using (var books = ko.Foreach(m => m.Books))
  {
    <tr>
      @using (var book = books.With(m => m))
      {
        <td @book.Bind.Text(m => m.Title)></td>
        <td @book.Bind.Text(m => m.Author)></td>
        <td @book.Bind.Text(m => m.Year)></td>
      }
    </tr>
  }
</table>
@ko.Apply(Model)
```

The **View** (Generated) will be as follows:

```
<table>
  <tr>
    <th>Title</th>
    <th>Author</th>
    <th>Year</th>
  </tr>
```

```
<!-- ko foreach: Books -->
    <tr>
<!-- ko with: $data -->
        <td data-bind="text : $data.Title"></td>
        <td data-bind="text : $data.Author"></td>
        <td data-bind="text : $data.Year"></td>
<!-- /ko -->
    </tr>
<!-- /ko -->
</table>
<script type="text/javascript">
var viewModelJs = {"Books":[{"Title":"Oliver Twist","Author":
  "Charles Dickens","Year":1837},{"Title":"Winnie-the-Pooh",
  "Author":"A. A. Milne","Year":1926},{"Title":"The Hobbit",
  "Author":"J. R. R. Tolkien","Year":1937}]};
var viewModel = ko.mapping.fromJS(viewModelJs);
ko.applyBindings(viewModel);
</script>
```

We defined the `book` variable using the following line:

```
@using (var book = books.With(m => m))
```

The preceding instruction transforms into the following:

```
<!-- ko with: $data -->
<!-- /ko -->
```

Now we can refer to the loop item via `$data`.

The if region

The `if` region allows you to use the `if` binding in an easy way. Let's update the library example with the "book read" status (read or unread) and the `if` region. Now each book row will include an additional field based on the read status.

The **Model** will be as follows:

```
public class BookModel
{
  public string Title { get; set; }
  public string Author { get; set; }
  public int Year { get; set; }
  public bool Read { get; set; }
}
```

```
public class LibraryModel
{
  public List<BookModel> Books { get; set; }
}
```

The **Controller** will be as follows:

```
public class LibraryController : KnockoutController
{
  public ActionResult Index()
  {
    var model = new LibraryModel
    {
      Books = new List<BookModel>
      {
        new BookModel { Title = "Oliver Twist", Author = "Charles
          Dickens", Year = 1837, Read = true },
        new BookModel { Title = "Winnie-the-Pooh", Author = "A. A.
          Milne", Year = 1926, Read = false },
        new BookModel { Title = "The Hobbit", Author = "J. R. R.
          Tolkien", Year = 1937, Read = true },
      }
    };
    return View(model);
  }
}
```

The **View** (Razor) will be as follows:

```
@using PerpetuumSoft.Knockout
@model KnockoutMvcDemo.Models.LibraryModel
@{
  var ko = Html.CreateKnockoutContext();
}
<table>
  <tr>
    <th>Title</th>
    <th>Author</th>
    <th>Year</th>
    <th>Read</th>
  </tr>
  @using (var books = ko.Foreach(m => m.Books))
  {
    <tr>
```

```
      @using (var book = books.With(m => m))
      {
        <td @book.Bind.Text(m => m.Title)></td>
        <td @book.Bind.Text(m => m.Author)></td>
        <td @book.Bind.Text(m => m.Year)></td>
        using (book.If(m => m.Read))
        {
          <td>Yes</td>
        }
        using (book.If(m => !m.Read))
        {
          <td>No</td>
        }
      }
    </tr>
  }
</table>
@ko.Apply(Model)
```

The **View** (Generated) will be as follows:

```
<table>
  <tr>
    <th>Title</th>
    <th>Author</th>
    <th>Year</th>
    <th>Read</th>
  </tr>
<!-- ko foreach: Books -->
    <tr>
<!-- ko with: $data -->
        <td data-bind="text : $data.Title"></td>
        <td data-bind="text : $data.Author"></td>
        <td data-bind="text : $data.Year"></td>
<!-- ko if: Read -->
          <td>Yes</td>
<!-- /ko -->
<!-- ko if: !Read() -->
          <td>No</td>
<!-- /ko -->
<!-- /ko -->
    </tr>
```

```
<!-- /ko -->
</table>
<script type="text/javascript">
var viewModelJs = {"Books":[{"Title":"Oliver Twist",
  "Author":"Charles Dickens","Year":1837,"Read":true},
  {"Title":"Winnie-the-Pooh","Author":"A. A. Milne",
  "Year":1926,"Read":false},{"Title":"The Hobbit","Author":
  "J. R. R. Tolkien","Year":1937,"Read":true}]};
var viewModel = ko.mapping.fromJS(viewModelJs);
ko.applyBindings(viewModel);
</script>
```

We used the `if` region of `book` twice with different conditions:

```
using (book.If(m => m.Read))
{
  <td>Yes</td>
}
using (book.If(m => !m.Read))
{
  <td>No</td>
}
```

The preceding code transforms into the following:

```
<!-- ko if: Read -->
  <td>Yes</td>
<!-- /ko -->
<!-- ko if: !Read() -->
  <td>No</td>
<!-- /ko -->
```

Thus the `if` region helps us create a conditional markup depending on the specified expressions.

Complex bindings

In some cases, we need to apply several bindings to a single element. This is easy to do; you just need to concatenate on the target binding methods. Let's update the previous example with the book read status. First, we set the binding for the status text with the `Text` method. Next, we set the color of the status: green for read books and red for unread books.

The **Model** will be as follows:

```
public class BookModel
{
  public string Title { get; set; }
  public string Author { get; set; }
  public int Year { get; set; }
  public bool Read { get; set; }
}
public class LibraryModel
{
  public List<BookModel> Books { get; set; }
}
```

The **Controller** will be as follows:

```
public class LibraryController : KnockoutController
{
  public ActionResult Index()
  {
    var model = new LibraryModel
    {
      Books = new List<BookModel>
      {
        new BookModel { Title = "Oliver Twist", Author = "Charles
          Dickens", Year = 1837, Read = true },
        new BookModel { Title = "Winnie-the-Pooh", Author = "A. A.
          Milne", Year = 1926, Read = false },
        new BookModel { Title = "The Hobbit", Author = "J. R. R.
          Tolkien", Year = 1937, Read = true },
      }
    };
    return View(model);
  }
}
```

The **View** (Razor) will be as follows:

```
@using PerpetuumSoft.Knockout
@model KnockoutMvcDemo.Models.LibraryModel
@{
  var ko = Html.CreateKnockoutContext();
}
<table>
  <tr>
```

```
      <th>Title</th>
      <th>Author</th>
      <th>Year</th>
      <th>Read</th>
    </tr>
    @using (var books = ko.Foreach(m => m.Books))
    {
      <tr>
        @using (var book = books.With(m => m))
        {
          <td @book.Bind.Text(m => m.Title)></td>
          <td @book.Bind.Text(m => m.Author)></td>
          <td @book.Bind.Text(m => m.Year)></td>
          <td @book.Bind.Text(m => m.Read ? "Yes" : "No").
            Style("color", m => m.Read ? "green" : "red")></td>
        }
      </tr>
    }
</table>
@ko.Apply(Model)
```

The **View** (Generated) will be as follows:

```
<table>
  <tr>
    <th>Title</th>
    <th>Author</th>
    <th>Year</th>
    <th>Read</th>
  </tr>
<!-- ko foreach: Books -->
    <tr>
<!-- ko with: $data -->
        <td data-bind="text : $data.Title"></td>
        <td data-bind="text : $data.Author"></td>
        <td data-bind="text : $data.Year"></td>
        <td data-bind="text : $data.Read() ? 'Yes' : 'No',style :
{color : $data.Read() ? 'green' : 'red'}"></td>
<!-- /ko -->
    </tr>
<!-- /ko -->
</table>
<script type="text/javascript">
```

```
var viewModelJs = {"Books":[{"Title":"Oliver Twist","Author":
  "Charles Dickens","Year":1837,"Read":true},{"Title":"Winnie-the-
  Pooh","Author":"A. A. Milne","Year":1926,"Read":false},
  {"Title":"The Hobbit","Author":"J. R. R. Tolkien",
  "Year":1937,"Read":true}]};
var viewModel = ko.mapping.fromJS(viewModelJs);
ko.applyBindings(viewModel);
</script>
```

As we can see, the target complex binding is set by the following line:

```
<td @book.Bind.Text(m => m.Read ? "Yes" : "No").Style("color", m
  => m.Read ? "green" : "red")></td>
```

The preceding line transforms into the following:

```
<td data-bind="text : $data.Read() ? 'Yes' : 'No',style :
  {color : $data.Read() ? 'green' : 'red'}"></td>
```

Sending parameters to the server

One of the common tasks in the development of responsive applications is the AJAX execution of a controller method. Sometimes, we need to execute the method with some parameters (or method arguments). Let's consider a simplified version of the library example; we will keep only the number of books. In the following example, the business model needs three methods: the addition of one book, the addition of two books, and the addition of three books. Of course, we can implement three different methods for these tasks. However, a single method with an argument is a more flexible approach.

The **Model** will be as follows:

```
public class LibraryModel
{
  public int AmountOfBooks { get; set; }

  public void AddBooks(int count)
  {
    AmountOfBooks += count;
  }
}
```

The **Controller** will be as follows:

```
public class LibraryController : KnockoutController
{
  public ActionResult Index()
  {
    return View(new LibraryModel());
  }

  public ActionResult AddBooks(LibraryModel model, int count)
  {
    model.AddBooks(count);
    return Json(model);
  }
}
```

The **View** (Razor) will be as follows:

```
@using PerpetuumSoft.Knockout
@model KnockoutMvcDemo.Models.LibraryModel
@{
  var ko = Html.CreateKnockoutContext();
}
Amount of books: @ko.Html.Span(m => m.AmountOfBooks)<br />
@ko.Html.Button("Add one book", "AddBooks", "Library", new { count
  = 1 })
@ko.Html.Button("Add two books", "AddBooks", "Library", new {
  count = 2 })
@ko.Html.Button("Add three books", "AddBooks", "Library", new {
  count = 3 })
@ko.Apply(Model)
```

The **View** (Generated) will be as follows:

```
Amount of books: <span data-bind="text : AmountOfBooks"></span><br
  />
<button data-bind="click : function() {executeOnServer(viewModel,
  &#39;/Library/AddBooks?count=1&#39;);}">Add one book</button>
<button data-bind="click : function() {executeOnServer(viewModel,
  &#39;/Library/AddBooks?count=2&#39;);}">Add two books</button>
<button data-bind="click : function() {executeOnServer(viewModel,
  &#39;/Library/AddBooks?count=3&#39;);}">Add three books</button>
<script type="text/javascript">
var viewModelJs = {"AmountOfBooks":0};
var viewModel = ko.mapping.fromJS(viewModelJs);
ko.applyBindings(viewModel);
</script>
```

In this example, we send the `count` parameter to the `AddBook` controller method by creating an anonymous object with the target value:

```
@ko.Html.Button("Add one book", "AddBooks", "Library", new { count
  = 1 })
@ko.Html.Button("Add two books", "AddBooks", "Library", new {
  count = 2 })
@ko.Html.Button("Add three books", "AddBooks", "Library", new {
  count = 3 })
```

Inner computed properties

Knockout MVC also supports simple computed properties. These properties have a JavaScript representation and can be calculated on the client without additional requests to the server. For example, let's define a computed property `DisplayText` for our `BookModel`. This property will be calculated on the basis of `Author` and `Title`.

The **Model** will be as follows:

```
public class BookModel
{
  public string Title { get; set; }
  public string Author { get; set; }

  [Computed]
  [ScriptIgnore]
  [JsonIgnore]
  public string DisplayText
  {
    get { return Author + ": " + Title; }
  }
}
public class LibraryModel
{
  public List<BookModel> Books { get; set; }
}
```

The **Controller** will be as follows:

```
public class LibraryController : KnockoutController
{
  public ActionResult Index()
  {
```

```
    var model = new LibraryModel
    {
      Books = new List<BookModel>
      {
        new BookModel { Title = "Oliver Twist", Author = "Charles
          Dickens" },
        new BookModel { Title = "Winnie-the-Pooh", Author = "A. A.
          Milne" },
        new BookModel { Title = "The Hobbit", Author = "J. R. R.
          Tolkien" },
      }
    };
    return View(model);
  }
}
```

The **View** (Razor) will be as follows:

```
@using PerpetuumSoft.Knockout
@model KnockoutMvcDemo.Models.LibraryModel
@{
  var ko = Html.CreateKnockoutContext();
}
<ul>
  @using (var books = ko.Foreach(m => m.Books))
  {
    <li>@books.Html.Span(m => m.DisplayText)</li>
  }
</ul>
@ko.Apply(Model)
```

The **View** (Generated) will be as follows:

```
<ul>
<!-- ko foreach: Books -->
    <li><span data-bind="text : $data.DisplayText"></span></li>
<!-- /ko -->
</ul>
<script type="text/javascript">
  var viewModelJs = {"Books":[{"Title":"Oliver Twist","Author":
    "Charles Dickens"},{"Title":"Winnie-the-Pooh","Author":
    "A. A. Milne"},{"Title":"The Hobbit","Author":"J. R. R.
    Tolkien"}]};
  var viewModelMappingData = {
```

```
    'Books': { create: function(options) {
      var data = ko.mapping.fromJS(options.data);
      data.DisplayText = ko.computed(function() { try { return
        ((this.Author() + ': ') + this.Title())} catch(e) { return
        null; }  ;}, data);
      return data;
    }}
  };
  var viewModel = ko.mapping.fromJS(viewModelJs,
    viewModelMappingData);
  ko.applyBindings(viewModel);
</script>
```

Note that we mark the `DisplayText` property with the following attributes: `Computed`, `ScriptIgnore`, and `JsonIgnore`. The first property tells Knockout MVC that we want to transform the corresponding `get` method into the Knockout.js computed property in the generated JavaScript code. The second and third properties tell Knockout MVC that we don't want to serialize data in the property (in the future version of the library, the set of attributes can be changed).

So, we defined a usual C# property with the `get` accessor:

```
public string DisplayText
{
  get { return Author + ": " + Title; }
}
```

The preceding code transforms into the following JavaScript logic:

```
data.DisplayText = ko.computed(function() { try { return
  ((this.Author() + ': ') + this.Title())} catch(e) { return null;
  }  ;}, data);
```

Now we can calculate `DisplayText` without an additional request to the server.

Multiple view models

Another important task in real projects is combining several views on the same page. In other words, you separated Models and their corresponding separated Views (in different files), but you want to display all Views at the same time. So, let's consider the following example.

The **Model** will be as follows:

```csharp
public class BookModel
{
  public string Title { get; set; }
  public string Author { get; set; }
}
public class LibraryModel
{
  public string LibraryName { get; set; }
  public List<BookModel> Books { get; set; }
}
public class ReaderModel
{
  public string FirstName { get; set; }
  public string LastName { get; set; }
  public BookModel FavoriteBook { get; set; }
}
public class MultipleViewModel
{
  public LibraryModel LibraryModel { get; set; }
  public ReaderModel ReaderModel { get; set; }
}
```

The **Controller** will be as follows:

```csharp
public class MultipleViewModelController : KnockoutController
{
  public ActionResult Index()
  {
    var model = new MultipleViewModel
    {
      LibraryModel = new LibraryModel
      {
        LibraryName = "Public library",
        Books = new List<BookModel>
            {
              new BookModel { Title = "Oliver Twist", Author =
                "Charles Dickens" },
              new BookModel { Title = "Winnie-the-Pooh", Author =
                "A. A. Milne" },
```

```
                        new BookModel { Title = "The Hobbit", Author = "J.
                            R. R. Tolkien" },
                    }
                },
                ReaderModel = new ReaderModel
                {
                    FirstName = "John",
                    LastName = "Doe",
                    FavoriteBook = new BookModel { Title = "The Green Mile",
                        Author = "Stephen King" }
                }
            };
            return View(model);
        }
    }
```

The **View** (Razor, `Index.cshtml`) will be as follows:

```
@model KnockoutMvcDemo.Models.MultipleViewModel
@Html.Partial("PartialLibraryView", Model.LibraryModel)
<hr />
@Html.Partial("PartialReaderView", Model.ReaderModel)
```

The **View** (Razor, `PartialLibraryView.cshtml`) will be as follows:

```
@using PerpetuumSoft.Knockout
@model KnockoutMvcDemo.Models.LibraryModel
@{
    var ko = Html.CreateKnockoutContext();
}
<div id="LibraryViewRootElement">
    <h3 @ko.Bind.Text(m => m.LibraryName)></h3>
    <table>
        <tr>
            <th>Title</th>
            <th>Author</th>
        </tr>
        @using (var books = ko.Foreach(m => m.Books))
        {
            <tr>
                <td @books.Bind.Text(book => book.Title)></td>
                <td @books.Bind.Text(book => book.Author)></td>
            </tr>
        }
    </table>
</div>
@ko.Apply(Model, "LibraryViewRootElement")
```

The **View** (Razor, `PartialReaderView.cshtml`) will be as follows:

```
@using PerpetuumSoft.Knockout
@model KnockoutMvcDemo.Models.ReaderModel
@{
  var ko = Html.CreateKnockoutContext();
}
<div id="ReaderViewRootElement">
  <h3>Reader</h3>
  <p>First name: @ko.Html.TextBox(m => m.FirstName)</p>
  <p>Last name: @ko.Html.TextBox(m => m.LastName)</p>
  <p>
    Favorite book:
    @using (var book = ko.With(m => m.FavoriteBook))
    {
      @book.Html.Span(m => m.Title);
      <span>(</span>@book.Html.Span(m => m.Author);<span>)</span>
    }
  </p>
</div>
@ko.Apply(Model, "ReaderViewRootElement")
```

The **View** (Generated) will be as follows:

```
<div id="LibraryViewRootElement">
  <h3 data-bind="text : LibraryName"></h3>
  <table>
    <tr>
      <th>Title</th>
      <th>Author</th>
    </tr>
<!-- ko foreach: Books -->
    <tr>
      <td data-bind="text : $data.Title"></td>
      <td data-bind="text : $data.Author"></td>
    </tr>
<!-- /ko -->
  </table>
</div>
<script type="text/javascript">
  var viewModelJs = {"LibraryName":"Public library",
    "Books":[{"Title":"Oliver Twist","Author":"Charles Dickens"},
    {"Title":"Winnie-the-Pooh","Author":"A. A. Milne"},{"Title":
    "The Hobbit","Author":"J. R. R. Tolkien"}]};
```

```
    var viewModel = ko.mapping.fromJS(viewModelJs);
    ko.applyBindings(viewModel, document.getElementById
      ('LibraryViewRootElement'))
</script>

<hr />
<div id="ReaderViewRootElement">
  <h3>Reader</h3>
  <p>First name: <input data-bind="value : FirstName"
    name="FirstName" type="text" /></p>
  <p>Last name: <input data-bind="value : LastName"
    name="LastName" type="text" /></p>
  <p>
    Favorite book:
<!-- ko with: FavoriteBook -->
<span data-bind="text : $data.Title"></span>
<span>(</span><span data-bind="text : $data.Author"
  ></span><span>)</span>
<!-- /ko -->
  </p>
</div>

<script type="text/javascript">
  var viewModelJs = {"FirstName":"John","LastName":
    "Doe","FavoriteBook":{"Title":"The Green Mile","Author":
    "Stephen King"}};
  var viewModel = ko.mapping.fromJS(viewModelJs);
  ko.applyBindings(viewModel, document.getElementById
    ('ReaderViewRootElement'))
</script>
```

In the preceding example, we have two models: `LibraryModel` and `ReaderModel`. The first model is a version of our usual model of a library. It contains the `LibraryName` property and the `Books` property (a collection of `BookModel`). The second model contains some data about a reader: `FirstName`, `LastName`, and `FavoriteBook`. Each model has its own View in a separate file. The corresponding Views have the named `div` elements (for example, `LibraryViewRootElement` for `LibraryModel`). We should use the name of this element in the Knockout MVC apply operation (for example, `@ko.Apply(Model, "LibraryViewRootElement")`).

Next, we have `MultipleViewModel` with two properties for our submodels and the corresponding controller. The main View (`Index.cshtml`) uses `@Html.Partial` to render partial views in specific places.

As a result, we have two complete Views (with personal Models) on the same page.

Lazy loading

In some cases, you have a big amount of data, and the page loading process needs time. A good practice is loading the full page markup first and then loading big data with an additional request to the server. Knockout MVC allows you do it in an easy way.

Imagine that your library contains a large number of books. Let's consider an example with lazy loading of the book list.

The **Model** will be as follows:

```
public class BookModel
{
  public string Title { get; set; }
  public string Author { get; set; }
}
public class LibraryModel
{
  public bool IsLoaded { get; set; }
  public List<BookModel> Books { get; set; }

  public void LoadData()
  {
    Books = new List<BookModel>();
    Books.Add(new BookModel { Title = "Oliver Twist", Author =
      "Charles Dickens" });
    Books.Add(new BookModel { Title = "Winnie-the-Pooh", Author =
      "A. A. Milne" });
    Books.Add(new BookModel { Title = "The Hobbit", Author = "J.
      R. R. Tolkien" });
    Thread.Sleep(2000); // Emulation of loading big book list
    IsLoaded = true;
  }
}
```

The **Controller** will be as follows:

```
public class LibraryController : KnockoutController
{
  public ActionResult Index()
  {
    return View();
  }
```

```
public ActionResult InitialData(LibraryModel model)
{
  model.LoadData();
  return Json(model);
}
}
```

The **View** (Razor) will be as follows:

```
@using PerpetuumSoft.Knockout
@model KnockoutMvcDemo.Models.LibraryModel
@{
  var ko = Html.CreateKnockoutContext();
}
<h3>Page header</h3>
<table>
  <tr>
    <th>Title</th>
    <th>Author</th>
  </tr>
  @using (ko.If(m => m.IsLoaded))
  {
    using (var books = ko.Foreach(m => m.Books))
    {
      <tr>
        @using (var book = books.With(m => m))
        {
          <td @book.Bind.Text(m => m.Title)></td>
          <td @book.Bind.Text(m => m.Author)></td>
        }
      </tr>
    }
  }
</table>
@ko.Html.Span("Loading...").Visible(m => !m.IsLoaded)
<h3>Page footer</h3>
@ko.LazyApply(Model, "InitialData", "Library")
```

The **View** (Generated) will be as follows:

```
<h3>Page header</h3>
<span data-bind="visible : !IsLoaded()">Loading...</span>
<table>
```

```
    <tr>
      <th>Title</th>
      <th>Author</th>
    </tr>
<!-- ko if: IsLoaded -->
<!-- ko foreach: Books -->
      <tr>
<!-- ko with: $data -->
            <td data-bind="text : $data.Title"></td>
            <td data-bind="text : $data.Author"></td>
<!-- /ko -->
      </tr>
<!-- /ko -->
<!-- /ko -->
</table>
<h3>Page footer</h3>

<script type="text/javascript">
  $(document).ready(function() {
    $.ajax({ url: '/Library/InitialData', type: 'POST', success:
      function (data) {
      var viewModel = ko.mapping.fromJS(data);
      ko.applyBindings(viewModel);
      }, error: function (error) { alert('There was an error
        posting the data to the server: ' + error.responseText); }
    });
  });
</script>
```

The Model has the additional `IsLoaded` property. Initially, it equals `false` and the book list is empty. Note that we used the `@ko.LazyApply(Model, "InitialData", "Library")` method instead of the usual `@ko.Apply` method. It means that Knockout MVC loads the full page at first and then executes the loading method (the second argument of `@ko.LazyApply`).

The View contains a special loading element:

```
@ko.Html.Span("Loading...").Visible(m => !m.IsLoaded)
```

It displays the "Loading..." label while `IsLoaded` equals `false`. Immediately after the data is loaded, the element will collapse (`Visible=false`). Instead, the content of the book table will be displayed because of the `if` region in the `@using (ko.If(m => m.IsLoaded))` statement.

Writing user scripts

Knockout MVC supports a large number of different methods that allow you to write the whole application in pure C# without any line of JavaScript code. However, sometimes we need to write some JavaScript code.

For example, say we want to create a button with the click logic that a title of each book should be enclosed in quotes. If the quote is already set at the beginning or end of the book title, we shouldn't add it again. Also, we will implement this logic in JavaScript on the client side.

The **Model** will be as follows:

```
public class BookModel
{
  public string Title { get; set; }
  public string Author { get; set; }
}
public class LibraryModel
{
  public List<BookModel> Books { get; set; }
}
```

The **Controller** will be as follows:

```
public class LibraryController : KnockoutController
{
  public ActionResult Index()
  {
    var model = new LibraryModel
    {
      Books = new List<BookModel>
      {
        new BookModel { Title = "Oliver Twist", Author = "Charles
          Dickens" },
        new BookModel { Title = "Winnie-the-Pooh", Author = "A. A.
          Milne" },
        new BookModel { Title = "The Hobbit", Author = "J. R. R.
          Tolkien" },
      }
    };
    return View(model);
  }
}
```

The **View** (Razor) will be as follows:

```
@using PerpetuumSoft.Knockout
@model KnockoutMvcDemo.Models.LibraryModel
@{
  var ko = Html.CreateKnockoutContext();
}

<table>
  <tr>
    <th>Title</th>
    <th>Author</th>
  </tr>
  @using (var books = ko.Foreach(m => m.Books))
  {
    <tr>
      <td @books.Bind.Text(book => book.Title)></td>
      <td @books.Bind.Text(book => book.Author)></td>
    </tr>
  }
</table>

<button data-bind="click: addQuotes">Add quotes</button>

@ko.Initialize(Model)
<script type="text/javascript">
  if (typeof String.prototype.startsWith != 'function') {
    String.prototype.startsWith = function (str) {
      return this.slice(0, str.length) == str;
    };
  }
  if (typeof String.prototype.endsWith != 'function') {
    String.prototype.endsWith = function (str) {
      return this.slice(-str.length) == str;
    };
  }

  viewModel.addQuotes = function () {
    for (var i = 0; i < viewModel.Books().length; i++) {
      var title = viewModel.Books()[i].Title();
      if (!title.startsWith("'"))
        title = "'" + title;
```

```
      if (!title.endsWith("'"))
        title = title + "'";
      viewModel.Books()[i].Title(title);
    }
  };
</script>
@ko.Apply(Model)
```

The **View** (Generated) will be as follows:

```
<table>
  <tr>
    <th>Title</th>
    <th>Author</th>
  </tr>
<!-- ko foreach: Books -->
    <tr>
      <td data-bind="text : $data.Title"></td>
      <td data-bind="text : $data.Author"></td>
    </tr>
<!-- /ko -->
</table>

<button data-bind="click: addQuotes">Add quotes</button>

<script type="text/javascript">
  var viewModelJs = {"Books":[{"Title":"Oliver Twist",
    "Author":"Charles Dickens"},{"Title":"Winnie-the-Pooh",
    "Author":"A. A. Milne"},{"Title":"The Hobbit","Author":"J. R.
    R. Tolkien"}]};
  var viewModel = ko.mapping.fromJS(viewModelJs);
</script>

<script type="text/javascript">
  if (typeof String.prototype.startsWith != 'function') {
    String.prototype.startsWith = function (str) {
      return this.slice(0, str.length) == str;
    };
  }
  if (typeof String.prototype.endsWith != 'function') {
    String.prototype.endsWith = function (str) {
      return this.slice(-str.length) == str;
    };
  }
```

```
viewModel.addQuotes = function () {
    for (var i = 0; i < viewModel.Books().length; i++) {
        var title = viewModel.Books()[i].Title();
        if (!title.startsWith("'"))
            title = "'" + title;
        if (!title.endsWith("'"))
            title = title + "'";
        viewModel.Books()[i].Title(title);
    }
};
</script>
<script type="text/javascript">
ko.applyBindings(viewModel);
</script>
```

The custom logic writing is very easy. You should split the @ko.Apply method into two calls: @ko.Initialize and @ko.Apply. You can place the custom JavaScript logic between these two calls and add any new properties to your ViewModel. In the preceding example, we added the addQuotes method in the JavaScript, and we added the <button data-bind="click: addQuotes">Add quotes</button> statement in the View. Therefore, a button click doesn't produce any request to the server and will be performed on the client.

Summary

In this chapter, you learned how to use some advanced features of Knockout MVC. One of the most useful features is regions, such as foreach, with, and if. Also, real-world applications often require that complex binding be made for some elements or that parameters be sent to the server via method arguments. Advanced applications may need to show several view models on the same page or make lazy data loading. Knockout MVC also supports all these features. It allows you to create very powerful and flexible web applications in pure C#. If you want to implement a part of the logic on the client and also avoid unnecessary requests to the server, you can use computed properties (also in pure C# — it will automatically transform into JavaScript) or write some custom JavaScript code.

A Brief on Knockout MVC References and Features

In this appendix, you will find a quick overview of the main Knockout MVC features. Most of the features are shown in the form of source Razor syntax and generated HTML/JavaScript output. You can use this appendix like a handbook while developing Knockout MVC applications.

Working with KnockoutContext

The main object when forming a View is an instance of the KnockoutContext class. It is necessary to create it at the beginning of the view, using the following line:

```
var ko = Html.CreateKnockoutContext();
```

At the end of the view, it is necessary to apply the formed data binding. You can do it in the following way:

```
@ko.Apply(Model)
```

If you have a lot of data that needs some time to load, it makes sense to use lazy analogue (in this case, a page will load first, and then an additional AJAX query will load all the data):

```
@ko.LazyApply(Model, "GetDataAction", "ControllerName")
```

So, a common view template looks like the following snippet of code:

```
@using PerpetuumSoft.Knockout
@model <!-- You model -->
@{
```

```
Html.CreateKnockoutContext();

ge -->

el)
```

..∪ data binding

It is possible to bind data by using `ko.Bind`. You can use a specific method of this object, which takes a lambda expression to specify the binding target. Both here and further on, we will show source Razor constructions and the resulting HTML code in the following way:

```
Razor: <span @ko.Bind.Text(m => m.MyText)>
Html:  <span data-bind="text: MyText">
```

It is possible to apply multiple data bindings to the element:

```
Razor: <span @ko.Bind.Text(m => m.MyText).Visible(m =>
  m.MyVisible).Style("fontSize", m => m.MyFontSize)>
Html:  <span data-bind="text: MyText, visible: MyVisible, style:
  {fontSize : MyFontSize}">
```

You can define the following properties by using data bindings (you can find more information in the official Knockout MVC specification):

- `Visible`: For this property, the example is as follows:

  ```
  Razor: @ko.Bind.Visible(m => m.MyVisible)
  Html:  data-bind="visible: myVisible"
  Razor: @ko.Bind.Visible(m => !Convert.ToBoolean(m.MyInt))
  Html:  data-bind="visible: !MyInt"
  ```

- `Text`: For this property, the example is as follows:

  ```
  Razor: @ko.Bind.Text(m => m.MyText)
  Html:  data-bind="text: MyText"
  ```

- `Html`: For this property, the example is as follows:

  ```
  Razor: @ko.Bind.Html(m => m.MyHtml)
  Html:  data-bind="html: MyHtml"
  ```

- `Value`: For this property, the example is as follows:

  ```
  Razor: @ko.Bind.Value(m => m.MyValue)
  Html:  data-bind="value: MyValue"
  ```

- `Disable`: For this property, the example is as follows:

  ```
  Razor: @ko.Bind.Disable(m => m.MyDisable)
  Html:  data-bind="disable: MyDisable"
  ```

- `Enable`: For this property, the example is as follows:

  ```
  Razor: @ko.Bind.Enable(m => m.MyEnable)
  Html:  data-bind="enable: MyEnable"
  ```

- `Checked`: For this property, the example is as follows:

  ```
  Razor: @ko.Bind.Checked(m => m.MyChecked)
  Html:  data-bind="checked: MyChecked"
  ```

- `Options`: For this property, the example is as follows:

  ```
  Razor: @ko.Bind.Options(m => m.MyOptions)
  Html:  data-bind="options: MyOptions"
  ```

- `SelectedOptions`: For this property, the example is as follows:

  ```
  Razor: @ko.Bind.SelectedOptions(m => m.MySelectedOptions)
  Html:  data-bind="selectedOptions: MySelectedOptions"
  ```

- `OptionsCaption`: For this property, the example is as follows:

  ```
  Razor: @ko.Bind.OptionsCaption(m => m.MyOptionsCaption)
  Html:  data-bind="optionsCaption: MyOptionsCaption"
  ```

- `Disable`: For this property, the example is as follows:

  ```
  Razor: @ko.Bind.Disable(m => m.MyDisable)
  Html:  data-bind="disable: MyDisable"
  ```

- `UniqueName`: For this property, the example is as follows:

  ```
  Razor: @ko.Bind.UniqueName()
  Html:  data-bind="uniqueName: true"
  ```

- `ValueUpdate`: For this property, the example is as follows:

  ```
  Razor: @ko.Bind.ValueUpdate(KnockoutValueUpdateKind.
    AfterKeyDown)
  Html:  data-bind="valueUpdate: afterkeydown"
  Razor: @ko.Bind.ValueUpdate(KnockoutValueUpdateKind.Change)
  Html:  data-bind="valueUpdate: change"
  Razor: @ko.Bind.ValueUpdate(KnockoutValueUpdateKind.KeyUp)
  Html:  data-bind="valueUpdate: keyup"
  Razor: @ko.Bind.ValueUpdate(KnockoutValueUpdateKind.
    KeyPress)
  Html:  data-bind="valueUpdate: keypress"
  ```

- Css: For this property, the example is as follows:

```
Razor: @ko.Bind.Css("class1", m => m.MyCondition1).
  Css("class2", m => m.MyCondition2)
Html:  data-bind="css: {class1: MyCondition1, class2:
  MyCondition2}"
```

- Style: For this property, the example is as follows:

```
Razor: @ko.Bind.Style("color", m => m.MyColor).
  Style("fontSize", m => m.MyFontSize)
Html:  data-bind="style: {color: MyColor, fontSize:
  MyFontSize}"
```

- Attr: For this property, the example is as follows:

```
Razor: @ko.Bind.Attr("href", m => m.MyHref).Attr("title", m
  => m.MyTitle)
Html:  data-bind="attr: {href: MyHref, title: MyTitle}"
```

- Click: For this property, the example is as follows:

```
Razor: @ko.Bind.Click("ActionName", "ControllerName", new {
  parameter = "Key" })
Html:  data-bind="click : function() {executeOnServer(
  viewModel, '/ControllerName/ActionName?parameter=Key');}"
```

The executeOnServer function is a helper function from the perpetuum. knockout.js (a Knockout MVC file), which wraps the jQuery AJAX call.

- Submit: For this property, the example is as follows:

```
Razor: @ko.Bind.Submit("ActionName", "ControllerName", new
  { parameter = "Key" })
Html:  data-bind="submit : function() {executeOnServer(
  viewModel, '/ControllerName/ActionName?parameter=Key');}"
```

- Custom: For this property, the example is as follows:

```
Razor: @ko.Bind.Custom("customName", m => m.MyCustom)
Html:  data-bind="customName: MyCustom"
```

Form objects

In this section, we will discuss some useful elements that will help you create HTML forms. You can create various form objects by using ko.Html, as shown in the preceding code. This approach is similar to the standard ASP MVC HTML helpers:

```
Razor: @ko.Html.TextBox(m => m.StringValue)
Html:  <input data-bind="value: StringValue" />
```

Every method has an optional parameter that defines a set of HTML attributes:

```
Razor: @ko.Html.RadioButton(m => m.RadioSelectedOptionValue, new {
  value = "Alpha" })
Html: <input data-bind="checked : RadioSelectedOptionValue"
  type="radio" value="Alpha" />
```

In addition, you can apply additional data bindings to the created objects:

```
Razor: @ko.Html.TextBox(m => m.StringValue).ValueUpdate
  (KnockoutValueUpdateKind.AfterKeyDown)
Html: <input data-bind="value : StringValue,valueUpdate :
  'afterkeydown'" />
```

You can create the following HTML objects:

- TextBox: For this object, the example is as follows:

  ```
  Razor: @ko.Html.TextBox(m => m.StringValue)
  Html: <input data-bind="value: StringValue" />
  ```

- Password: For this object, the example is as follows:

  ```
  Razor: @ko.Html.Password(m => m.PasswordValue)
  Html: <input data-bind="value: StringValue" type=
    "password"/>
  ```

- Hidden: For this object, the example is as follows:

  ```
  Razor: @ko.Html.Hidden()
  Html: <input type="hidden"/>
  ```

- RadioButton: For this object, the example is as follows:

  ```
  Razor: @ko.Html.RadioButton(m => m.
    RadioSelectedOptionValue)
  Html: <input data-bind="value: StringValue" type="radio"/>
  ```

- CheckBox: For this object, the example is as follows:

  ```
  Razor: @ko.Html.CheckBox(m => m.BooleanValue)
  Html: <input data-bind="value: StringValue" type=
    "checkbox"/>
  ```

- TextArea: For this object, the example is as follows:

  ```
  Razor: @ko.Html.TextArea(m => m.StringValue)
  Html: <textarea data-bind="value : StringValue">
    </textarea>
  ```

- `DropDownList`: For this object, the example is as follows:

```
Razor: @ko.Html.DropDownList(m => m.OptionValue)
Html:  <select data-bind="options : OptionValue"></select>
Razor: @ko.Html.DropDownList(m => m.OptionValue, null, item
  => item.Key)
Html:  <select data-bind="options : OptionValue,
  optionsText : function(item) { return item.Key; }">
  </select>
Razor: @ko.Html.DropDownList(m => m.OptionValue, null, (m,
  item) => m.Prefix + item.Key)
Html:  <select data-bind="options : OptionValue,
  optionsText : function(item) { return Prefix + item.Key;
  }"></select>
```

- `ListBox`: For this object, the example is as follows:

```
Razor: @ko.Html.ListBox(m => m.OptionValue)
Html:  <select data-bind="options : OptionValue" multiple=
  "multiple"></select>
Razor: @ko.Html.ListBox(m => m.OptionValue, null, item =>
  item.Key)
Html:  <select data-bind="options : OptionValue,
  optionsText : function(item) { return item.Key; }"
  multiple="multiple"></select>
Razor: @ko.Html.ListBox(m => m.OptionValue, null, (m, item)
  => m.Prefix + item.Key)
Html:  <select data-bind="options : OptionValue,
  optionsText : function(item) { return Prefix + item.Key;
  }" multiple="multiple"></select>
```

- `Span`: For this object, the example is as follows:

```
Razor: @ko.Html.Span(m => m.StringValue)
Html:  <span data-bind="text: StringValue"></span>
Razor: @ko.Html.Span("text")
Html:  <span>text</span>
```

- `SpanInline`: For this object, the example is as follows:

```
Razor: @ko.Html.SpanInline("new Date().getSeconds()")
Html:  <span data-bind="text : new Date().
  getSeconds()"></span>
```

 The `SpanInline` method takes a string and pastes it in the `text` binding of span elements. You can use it for an explicit JavaScript code. The `Span` method can take a lambda expression (and process it in the usual Knockout MVC way) or string (and paste it inside the span element instead of a binding value).

- Button: For this object, the example is as follows:

```
Razor: @ko.Html.Button("Caption", "ActionName",
   "ControllerName", new { parameter = "Key"})
Html:   <button data-bind="click : function()
   {executeOnServer(viewModel, '/ControllerName/
   ActionName?parameter=Key');}">Caption</button>
```

- HyperlinkButton: For this object, the example is as follows:

```
Razor: @ko.Html.HyperlinkButton("Caption", "ActionName",
   "ControllerName", new { parameter = "Key"})
Html:   <a href="#" data-bind="click : function()
   {executeOnServer(viewModel, '/ControllerName/
   ActionName?parameter=Key');}">Caption</a>
```

- Form: For this object, the example is as follows:

```
Razor: @using (ko.Html.Form("ActionName", "ControllerName",
   new { parameter = "Key"}))
      {
        Text
      }
Html:   <form data-bind="submit : function()
   {executeOnServer(viewModel, '/ControllerName/
   ActionName?parameter=Key');}">
        Text
      </form>
```

Nested contexts

Nested contexts allow developers to wrap a part of a view in a special construction, which offers some additional behavior.

It is possible to create the following types of nested contexts:

- Foreach: This nested context walks through all collection elements and provides easy access to HTML elements:

```
Razor: @using (var items = ko.Foreach(m => m.Items))
      {
        <tr>
          <td @items.Bind.Text(items.GetIndex())>
          </td>
          <td @items.Bind.Text(m => m)>
          </td>
        </tr>
      }
```

Appendix

```
                                   Items -->

                                     "text : $index()">

                                     'text : $data">
```

to a subentity of the main model:

```
                                 = ko.With(m => m.SubModel))

                                 lel = subModel.With(m =>


                         _.html.Span(m => ko.Model.ModelName +
                       " " + subModel.Model.SubModelName + " " +
                      m.SubSubModelName)
                  }
              }
Html:   <!-- ko with: SubModel -->
          <!-- ko with: SubSubModel -->
            <span data-bind="text : $parents[1].
              ModelName()+' '+$parent.SubModelName()+'
              '+SubSubModelName()"></span>
          <!-- /ko -->
        <!-- /ko -->
```

- `If`: With this, some elements will be displayed according to a specified condition:

```
Razor: @using (ko.If(model => model.Condition1 || model.
  Condition2))
        {
          <p>Text</p>
        }
Html:   <!-- ko if: Condition1()||Condition2() -->
          <p>Text</p>
        <!-- /ko -->
```

Sending requests to the server

It is assumed that the main logic of the model processing is hosted on the server. Every action that we perform on the model should correspond to a method in the controller:

```
public class FooController : KnockoutController {
  public ActionResult FooAction(FooModel model)
  {
    model.FooAction();
    return Json(model);
  }
}
```

As you can see from the preceding example, the method takes the model parameter that the main model sent from the client side. ASP.NET maps it to a C# object. In other words, the model parameter contains the status of the client model at the time of sending. It is possible to perform the necessary manipulations on the model and send the updated model in the JSON format with help of return Json(model);. You should pay attention to the fact that the base class for the controller is KnockoutController. This base class contains the extended logic to work with the JSON format.

For example, you can create a special control to send requests to the server:

```
Razor: @ko.Html.Button("Display", "FooAction", "Foo")
Html:  <button data-bind="click : function() {executeOnServer
  (viewModel, '/FooController/FooAction');}">Display</button>

Razor: @ko.Html.HyperlinkButton("Display", "FooAction", "Foo")
Html:  <a href="#" data-bind="click : function()
  {executeOnServer(viewModel, '/FooController/FooAction');}
  ">Display</a>

Razor: @using (ko.Html.Form("FooAction", "Foo"))
       {
         Display
       }
Html:  <form data-bind="submit : function() {executeOnServer
  (viewModel, '/FooController/FooAction');}">
       Display
       </form>
```

It is possible to insert the request code directly into the page:

```
<script type="text/javascript">
  function foo() {
    @ko.ServerAction("FooAction", "Foo");
  }
</script>
```

All these constructions can be extended with some parameters:

```
public class FooController : KnockoutController {
  public ActionResult FooParametersAction(FooModel model, int
    value, string name)
  {
    model.FooParametersAction(value, name);
    return Json(model);
  }
}
```

Razor: @ko.Html.Button("Display", "FooParametersAction", "Foo",
  new { value = 0, name = "Sanderson"})
Html: <button data-bind="click : function() {executeOnServer
  (viewModel, '/FooController/FooParametersAction?value=0
  &name=Sanderson');}">Display</button>

Razor: @ko.Html.HyperlinkButton("Display", "FooParametersAction",
  "Foo", new { value = 0, name = "Sanderson"})
Html: <a href="#" data-bind="click : function() {executeOnServer
  (viewModel, '/FooController/FooParametersAction?value=0
  &name=Sanderson');}">Display</a>

Razor: @using (ko.Html.Form("FooParametersAction", "Foo", new {
  value = 0, name = "Sanderson"}))
        {
          Display
        }
Html: <form data-bind="submit : function() {executeOnServer
  (viewModel, '/FooController/FooParametersAction?value=0
  &name=Sanderson');}">
          Display
        </form>

```
<script type="text/javascript">
  function foo() {
    @ko.ServerAction("FooParametersAction", "Foo", new { value =
      0, name = "Sanderson"});
  }
</script>
```

Adding user-defined scripts

If necessary, you can add your own Knockout.js code to the automatically generated code. It is important to initialize the generated model with the following code:

```
@ko.Initialize(Model)
```

This method will create a model named `viewModel` and fill it with data that is taken from the `Model` parameter. Then, you can add custom JavaScript code and extend a model:

```
<script type="text/javascript">
  viewModel.someProperty = someValue;
</script>
```

After the necessary custom script is added, you should activate Knockout with the following code:

```
@ko.Apply(Model)
```

Forming a model and using computed properties

In addition to having the opportunity to bind interface elements to specific model properties, you can also bind them to expressions. Let's look at some examples:

```
Razor: <button type="submit" @ko.Bind.Enable(m => m.
  StringValue.Length > 0)>Add</button>
Html:  <button type="submit" data-bind="enable : StringValue().
  length>0">Add</button>


Razor: @ko.Bind.Enable(m => m.Items.Count > 0)
Html:  data-bind="enable : Items().length>0"


Razor: @using (ko.If(model => model.Condition1 && model.
  Condition2))
Html:  <!-- ko if: Condition1()&&Condition2() -->


Razor: @ko.Html.Span(m => m.Price).Style("color", m => m.Price > 0
  ? "black" : "red")
Html:  <span data-bind="text : Price,style : {color : Price()>0 ?
  'black' : 'red'}"></span>
```

Also, you can create computed properties directly as a model part:

```
C#: public Expression<Func<string>> FullName() { return () =>
   FirstName + " " + LastName; }
Html:  viewModel.FullName = ko.computed(function() { try { return
   this.FirstName()+' '+this.LastName()} catch(e) { return null; }
   ;}, viewModel);
```

As you can see from the preceding example, the standard `viewModel` will be extended with a special computed property. The advantage of such an approach is that the declared method can be used not only on the server side, but also as a data binding on the client side:

```
Razor: @ko.Html.Span(m => m.FullName())
Html:  <span data-bind="text : FullName"></span>
```

Special addressing forms

In the Knockout.js library, there are some specific keywords you will use.
Let's review their Knockout MVC analogue:

- `$parent`, `$parents`, `$root`, and `$parentContext`: These properties allow you to refer to different data binding contexts. You don't need think about the scopes hierarchy and peculiarities of addressing between them in Knockout MVC—now every context has a name! Consider the following code snippet:

```
Razor: @using (var items = ko.Foreach(m => m.Items))
       {
          using (var subItems = items.Foreach(m =>
            m.SubItems))
          {
            @subItems.Html.Span(m => ko.Model.Key + " " +
              items.Model.Caption + " " + m.Name)<br />
          }
       }
Html:  <!-- ko foreach: Items -->
          <!-- ko foreach: SubItems -->
            <span data-bind="text : $parents[1].Key()+'
              '+$parent.Caption()+' '+Name()"></span><br />
          <!-- /ko -->
          <!-- /ko -->
```

- `$index`: This makes it possible to get an index of a collection element in the `Foreach` context. You can use the `GetIndex()` function to get the corresponding property of each context:

```
Razor: @using (var items = ko.Foreach(m => m.Items))
       {
           <span @items.Bind.Text(items.GetIndex())></span>
       }
Html:  <!-- ko foreach: Items -->
           <span data-bind="text : $index()"></span>
       <!-- /ko -->
```

- `$data`: This makes it possible to get a collection element in the `Foreach` context. In the Knockout MVC, you just should create a lambda expression that will map a model to itself, as shown here:

```
Razor: @using (var items = ko.Foreach(m => m.Items))
       {
           <span @items.Bind.Text(m => m)></span>
       }
Html:  <!-- ko foreach: Items -->
           <span data-bind="text : $data()"></span>
       <!-- /ko -->
```

Summary

You can also find the full documentation on the official site at http://knockoutmvc.com/Home/Documentation.

Remember, Knockout MVC is not suited for all kinds of Knockout.js-based projects. The Knockout MVC library can be very useful for some simple applications. It can help you to write applications easy and quickly. However, it has some important limitations. If you want to develop a very big and complex application, you should perhaps use vanilla Knockout.js without additional wrappers. Briefly recall Knockout MVC pro et contra.

Knockout MVC can be useful if you need an easy way to create a client-server web application without writing JavaScript code, if you want to have syntax checking and type checking on the compilation stage, or if all of your data processing methods should perform on the server side.

You probably don't need Knockout MVC if you have a big model and you don't want to send the entire model on each request, or if you want to implement a part of the logic only on the client side.

Be careful when you choose the target library. You should clearly understand the advantages and disadvantages of Knockout MVC.

Index

Thank you for buying
Getting Started with Knockout.js
for .NET Developers

About Packt Publishing

Packt, pronounced 'packed', published its first book, *Mastering phpMyAdmin for Effective MySQL Management*, in April 2004, and subsequently continued to specialize in publishing highly focused books on specific technologies and solutions.

Our books and publications share the experiences of your fellow IT professionals in adapting and customizing today's systems, applications, and frameworks. Our solution-based books give you the knowledge and power to customize the software and technologies you're using to get the job done. Packt books are more specific and less general than the IT books you have seen in the past. Our unique business model allows us to bring you more focused information, giving you more of what you need to know, and less of what you don't.

Packt is a modern yet unique publishing company that focuses on producing quality, cutting-edge books for communities of developers, administrators, and newbies alike. For more information, please visit our website at www.packtpub.com.

About Packt Open Source

In 2010, Packt launched two new brands, Packt Open Source and Packt Enterprise, in order to continue its focus on specialization. This book is part of the Packt Open Source brand, home to books published on software built around open source licenses, and offering information to anybody from advanced developers to budding web designers. The Open Source brand also runs Packt's Open Source Royalty Scheme, by which Packt gives a royalty to each open source project about whose software a book is sold.

Writing for Packt

We welcome all inquiries from people who are interested in authoring. Book proposals should be sent to author@packtpub.com. If your book idea is still at an early stage and you would like to discuss it first before writing a formal book proposal, then please contact us; one of our commissioning editors will get in touch with you.

We're not just looking for published authors; if you have strong technical skills but no writing experience, our experienced editors can help you develop a writing career, or simply get some additional reward for your expertise.

KnockoutJS Starter

ISBN: 978-1-78216-114-1   Paperback: 50 pages

Learn how to knock out your next app in no time with KnockoutJS

1. Learn something new in an Instant! A short, fast, focused guide delivering immediate results.

2. Learn how to develop a deployable app as the author walks you through each step.

3. Understand how to customize and extend KnockoutJS to take your app to the next level.

Instant Ext JS Starter

ISBN: 978-1-78216-610-8   Paperback: 56 pages

Find out what Ext JS actually is, what you can do with it, and why it's so great

1. Learn something new in an Instant! A short, fast, focused guide delivering immediate results.

2. Install and set up the environment with this quick Starter guide.

3. Learn the basics of the framework and built-in utility functions.

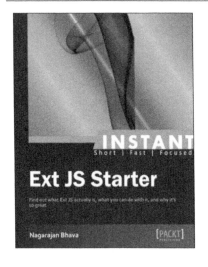

Please check **www.PacktPub.com** for information on our titles

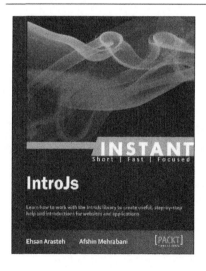